ASANTE - OLD TESTAMENT SACRIFICIAL SYSTEMS
A Comparative Analysis of the Concept of *Asham* Reparation Sacrifice between the Old Testament and the Asante Sacrificial System

by

Noah Aboagye Osei

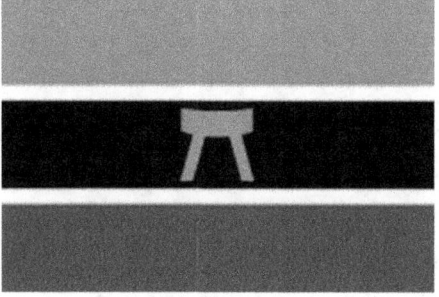

Asante Flag

HCU Media LLC
Accra, Ghana • Richardson, TX

ASANTE-OLD TESTAMENT SACRIFICIAL SYSTEMS

A COMPARATIVE ANALYSIS OF THE CONCEPT OF ASHAM REPARATION SACRIFICE BETWEEN THE OLD TESTAMENT AND THE ASANTE SACRIFICIAL SYSTEM

HCU Media LLC
www.HCUMedia.com

Commemorative Edition –
Published and Copyright © 2016
By Noah Aboagye Osei & HCU Media LLC

ISBN-13: 978-1-939468-05-5 (Paperback Edition)
Also available in paperback & Kindle form on Amazon.com

ALL RIGHTS RESERVED
No part of this publication may be reproduced, stored in a retrieval system, or transmitted in any form by any means – electronic, mechanical, photocopying, recording or otherwise – without prior written consent.

Cover Design by Dale Henry – www.dalehenrydesign.com

Commemorative Edition June 2016
10 9 8 7 6 5 4 3 2 1

This study reflects the research done by Mr. Noah Aboagye Osei in fulfillment of a MA degree in Old Testament in the Graduate School of Theology, College of Biblical Studies, Abilene Christian University, Abilene, Texas, USA, 2014.

Acknowledgements

This book is presented to my wife Agatha, and children Mae, Nana, and Kofi in sincere appreciation for their perseverance, encouragement, and support during the research and writing of this work. I would also like to use this opportunity to express my profound gratitude to Yahweh the Almighty for his faithfulness. I am indebted to the following individuals for their invaluable contribution towards the completion of this study; Dr. James Thompson who advised me to enroll in this program; Dr. Mark Hamilton my supervisor, for his patience and constructive contributions; Dr. John Willis and Dr. Christopher Flanders for their inspiration, encouragement and opening their doors to me anytime I needed help.

My thanks go to Dr. Samuel Twumasi-Ankrah the president of Heritage Christian College and the Heritage Christian College Foundation, USA and Ghana for their moral and spiritual support especially Mr. Deon Fair who encouraged me to undertake the Old Testament course. I acknowledge the efforts of Mr. Craig Churchill, the ACU Library staff, ACU Team 55, and the faculty and staff of the Graduate School of Theology, especially Madam LaCresha Longwell.

Also, I appreciate the effort of my good friend Lonnie Meredith and the Haskell Church of Christ for their spiritual support. I thank the Wylie Church of Christ, Abilene, Texas, for their incessant prayers for the success of this project work.

My sincere appreciation also goes to all those whose names I could not mention but who have contributed immensely in many ways to the success of my research.

Comments from reviewers:

"A major task of Christian theology today is to address concerns arising in the Global South. In this thought-provoking work, Noah Osei recovers an often neglected part of the biblical tradition itself – the practice of sacrifice – and explores similarities and differences between the Bible and traditional African religions. Along the way, he opens doors to new theological work that can inform both Africans and all the rest of us. He reminds us that the spirit-body division so common in Western theology is alien to the Bible itself and the source of many misunderstandings of Christianity. I recommend this work as a starting point for what should be a long and rich conversation."
Dr. Mark Hamilton, Professor of Old Testament, Graduate School of Theology, Abilene Christian University (ACU)

"An insightful comparative study of two traditions (Akan and Jewish)."
Dr. Daniel A. Obiri-Yeboah, Senior Lecturer, School of Business and Management, Dept. of Liberal Studies, Accra Polytechnic, Accra.

"This masterpiece demonstrates the universality of human cultures"
Dr. Ebenezer Ayesu, Senior Research Fellow, Institute of African Studies, University of Ghana, Legon.

About the author

Mr. Noah Aboagye Osei, Lecturer, Heritage Christian College (www.hcc.edu.gh), MA in Old Testament, Abilene Christian University, Abilene TX, USA (www.acu.edu), MA in Agricultural Administration, University of Ghana (www.ug.edu.gh), and a Bachelor of Religious Education (BRE), Acadia University, Canada (www2.acadia.ca]

Contents

Hebrew Sacrificial Terms i

Abstract ii

Abbreviations iv

Chapter 1: Introduction 1

Chapter 2: Asham Sacrifice in Israel 19

Chapter 3: Asham Sacrifice in Asante Traditional Religion. 41

Chapter 4: Similarities and Dissimilarities 75

Chapter 5: Conclusion and Recommendations 89

Select Bibliography 91

Asante Ritual Symbols and Images 97

Hebrew Sacrificial Terms

Asham - Guilt/ Reparation Offering (Lev 5:6)
Chattat - Sin Offering (Lev 5:6)
Asham – Asante Reparation Sacrifices or guilt appeasement offerings.

Lev 5:5, 6. "*⁵ When a man is guilty in any of these, he shall confess the sin he has committed, ⁶ and he shall bring his guilt offering (asham) to the LORD for the sin which he has committed, a female from the flock, a lamb or a goat, for a sin offering (chattat); and the priest shall make atonement for him for his sin.*"

Abstract

This study aims at a number of objectives such as examining the concept of expiatory sacrifice, particularly the *āšām, asham, guilt offering* in Leviticus (Lev 5:14-19; 6:1-7; 7:1-8; 14:12, 24, 25; 19:20-22), and the Asante tradition. It compares the concept of so-called "guilt" sacrifice as it is understood in the two religions and after identifying the similarities and dissimilarities of guilt sacrifices between the two religions, exploring the means by which a thorough understanding of the concept can be used in furthering the gospel of Christ.

This study is a comparative study of the asham sacrificial concepts of the Israelites (Jews) of the Old Testament times and the contemporary Asante religion of the Asante people of Ghana in West Africa.

The study which compares the sacrificial practices of the two religions, is a response to a theological struggle of Christian evangelism among Asantes and for that matter Ghanaians. Often scholars of the Asante traditional religion point out that sacrifices in the Old Testament share similar features with the Asante Traditional religion andthat the attributes of the Christian God are not different from the Supreme God of the Asantes.[1] This world view of the Asante traditionalist is intensifying to the extent that conversion to Christianity is becoming a challenging evangelistic effort. This study is missiologically significant then as it attempts to ascertain the similarities and the dissimilarities of guilt sacrifice in the two religions, and to recommend ways in which they may interact.

This study draws on the scholarly works of Mary Douglas,[2] Jacob Milgrom,[3] both scholars of the book of Leviticus, and Peter

---

[1] Asante traditional term (Oral Tradition).
[2] Mary Douglas, *Leviticus As Literature,* (Oxford: Oxford University Press, 1999).
[3] Jacob Milgrom, *Leviticus 1-16(AB 3:* (New York: Doubleday, 1991).

K. Sarpong,[4] K. A. Busia,[5] scholars of the Asante culture, and numerous other scholars to accomplish the aim of this project. The author employs personal knowledge and observations regarding some Asante religious activities which correspond with the results of personal interviews with some Asante chiefs who are the custodians of the Asante traditional religious heritage.

The results from the study show that there are similar ideas that the Israelite and the Asante religions have on guilt sacrifice. However, the reality must not be overlooked that there are significant differences in the practice of each of the religions.

Even though the Israelites and Asante are similar in some of their religious concepts, they are dissimilar in reality and practice. This study has revealed and confirmed the fact that Yahweh made humans and breathed His spirit in them so they could understand the sacredness of the spiritual realm.

---

[4] Peter Sarpong, *Ghana in Retrospect: Some Aspect of Ghanaian Culture*, (Tema, Ghana: Ghana Publishing Corporation, 1974).
[5] K. A. Busia, *The Position of the chief in the Modern Political System of Ashanti*, (Oxford: Oxford University Press, 1951).

Abbreviations

AB	*Anchor Bible*
AFE	*African Ecclesial Review*
BDBF.	Brown, S. R. Driver, and C. A. Briggs. *A Hebrew and English Lexicon of the Old Testament.*
EuroJTh	*The European Journal of Theology*
FIR	*Fieldwork in Religion*
JBL	*Journal of Biblical Literature*
JSAH	*Journal of the Society of Architectural Historians*
JSOT	*Journal for the Study of the Old Testament*
MAQ	*Medical Anthropology Quarterly*
NIDOTTE	*New International Dictionary of New Testament Theology and Exegesis.* Edited by W. A. VanGemeren. 5 vols. Grand Rapids, 1997
SBL	*Society of Biblical Literature*

Chapter 1: Introduction

This study has the following objectives:
- to examine the concept of the *Asham* Sacrifice in Leviticus (Lev 5:14-19; 6:1-7; 7:1-8; 14:12, 24, 25; 19:20-22) and that of the Asante Religion.
- to compare the concepts of *Asham* Sacrifice as it is understood in the two religions.
- to identify the similarities and dissimilarities of *Asham* Sacrifices between the two religions,
- to explore the means by which a thorough understanding of the concept can be used in the preaching of the gospel of Christ.

By examining a single aspect of a much larger set of issues as it compares the *asham* sacrifice in the Israelite and the Asante religions and drawing out the similarities and dissimilarities between the two religions, the study plans to lay a foundation for ongoing theological reflection in an Asante context. Perhaps future studies will consider developing a Christian theology in the context of the Asante religious values and ideas as well as the other aspects relating to the study.

In part, this study, which compares the sacrificial practices of the two religions, is a response to a theological struggle of Christian evangelism among Asantes and for that matter Ghanaians. Scholars, Asante Christian converts and adherents of Asante Traditional religion point out that the concept of sacrifices found in the Old Testament, share similar features with the Asante Traditional religion and that the attributes of the Christian God are not different from the Supreme God of the Asantes.[6] This world view of the Asante traditionalists is intensifying to the extent that conversion to Christianity is becoming a challenging evangelistic effort. This study is missiologically significant then, as it attempts to ascertain the similarities and the dissimilarities of *asham* sacrifice in the two religions and to recommend ways in which they may interact. In discerning their interaction, we need to understand the nature and functions of sacrifice, as the next section of

---
[6] Asante traditional term (Oral Tradition).

this study will demonstrate. Thus, this chapter discusses several approaches to sacrifice, the study's literature reviews, a methodology for the study, and the specific study of sacrifice in general.

The Conceptual and Theoretical Framework
The Nature and Functions of Sacrifice

Sacrifice is a ritual that has had numerous functions varying from place to place and society to society. Labelle Prussin regards sacrifice as one of the elements that strengthens ties between people: "Every sacrifice reinforces the group's solidarity."[7] Certain cultures, like the Dagomba in the northern part of Ghana, believe sacrifice to be the power behind every effective herbal healing. This is because they believe that the efficacy of plant medicines is derived from the ancestors. Bernhard Bierlich says, "The production of botanical substances involves a sacrifice or the pouring of libations accompanied by prayers."[8] Similarly, there are certain trees and plant leaves that some of the traditional herbal medicine practitioners known as "herbalists" in Asante believe accommodate a specific kind of spirit. So the bark of a specific tree or the leaf of a plant cannot be picked without a sacrifice or money put under the tree.

According to Henri Hubert and Marcel Mauss, sacrifice always implies a consecration, for in every sacrifice an object passes from the common into the sacred domain. In sacrifice, the consecration extends beyond the thing consecrated, among other objects; it touches the moral person who bears the expenses of the ceremony. At the end of the sacrifice, the person sacrificing has acquired a new religious character or gotten rid of an unfavorable characteristic. The person has entered a state of grace or has emerged from a state of sin. Therefore, sacrifice produces a double effect: *first*, the effect on the object for which it is offered

---

[7] Labelle Prussin, "Non-Western Sacred Sites; African Models" *JSAH* 58.3 (1999/2000): 424-433.
[8] Bernhard Bierlich, "Sacrifice, Plants, and Western Pharmaceuticals: Money and Health care in Northern Ghana," *MAQ*, New Series 13. 13 (Sep. 1999): 316-37.

and upon which it is desired to act; and *second* on the moral person who desires and instigates that effect.⁹ This means that sacrifice results in religious transformation.

In this chapter, as already noted, the study will discuss some approaches to sacrifice, such as the socio-anthropological approach, the African tradition approach, and the Biblical view of sacrifice. Also, the study will present the theories of Bernhard Lang and Adolf E. Jensen on sacrifice. Again, it will discuss the literature reviewed, the research methodology, and the organization of the study. Furthermore, there will be discussion on the Israelite sacrifice, the *asham* sacrifice in Leviticus, the Asante sacrifice, the *asham* sacrifice in Asante, and draw some conclusions. It will begin first with some approaches to sacrifice.

Approaches to Sacrifice

Like beauty in the eye of the beholder, sacrifice appears to scholars in various fields related to human socio-cultural and religious activities to be easy to spot but difficult to define. As Jack Glazier notes, anthropologists and historians have viewed sacrifice variously as a gift to the gods, a substitute for the killing of divine kings whose powers were waning, and/or the common meal that joined congregants with a god or other divine power.¹⁰ It is clear that the word *sacrifice* has more than one meaning and tends to create confusion if one is not careful. As Norman Snaith puts it, "Writers tend to start with one meaning for the word, and finish with another. The word *sacrificial* has a host of meanings in our English tongue, and many of those who use the word are not careful enough of their exact meaning."¹¹ This study presents the socio-anthropological approach, the African traditional approach, and the biblical approach: This begins with the socio-anthropological approach.

The Socio-Anthropological Approach.

Snaith explains that, "The strict derivative meaning of the Latin *Sacrificium* is to make a *sacer,* which is to bring something

---

[9] Henri Hubert and Marcel Mauss, *Sacrifice: Its Nature and Function* (Trans. W.D. Halls; Chicago: University of Chicago Press, 1964), 9-11.
[10] Jack Glazier, "Sacrifice," *Encyclopedia of Cultural Anthropology* 4:1133.
[11] Norman Snaith. *Mercy and Sacrifice,* (London: SCM, 1953), 102.

or someone within the realm or orbit of the *sacer*. *Sacer* is that which is consecrated or belongs to divinity, that which is "holy." Therefore, "*Sacrificium* is that which is brought or has come to be within the sphere of holy things and it may refer to any action in the cultus or anything or person connected with the shrine or the Deity."[12] He also says that:

> The word holy has to do with the Otherness of things, that non-visible, suprahuman world by which early human beings believed themselves to be on every side surrounded. Holiness assumes a *mysterium tremendum,* the mysterium refers to the Wholly Other, and elements of tremendum include awefulness, overpoweringness and urgency.[13]

African Tradition

According to Deji Ayegboyin, sacrifice may be defined as the "giving up" of a thing for the sake of another that is higher or more urgent. Sacrifice is for the purpose of maintaining or restoring a right relationship of human beings to the sacred order.[14]

> In the African Traditional Religion, the greater and more urgent the need for maintenance, restoration and enhancement of any broken relationship, the more worthy the victim an African was prepared to give. In the religious realm, sacrifice is an act of relinquishing or offering a consecrated object or victim for the moral and spiritual benefit of the individual or group concerned. It is a means of restoring the *theoanthropic* relationship (between God and people). When good relationship exists between human beings and the supernatural powers, the former express their gratitude to the latter through sacrifices of thanksgiving, votive or communion. But when the relationship is sour, expiatory, placatory or substitutionary sacrifices are offered in an attempt to restore the congenial relationship.[15]

---

[12] Ibid. 103.
[13] Ibid. 104.
[14] Deji Ayegboyin, "Sacrifice," *Encyclopedia of African Religion.* 2.583.
[15] J.O. Ubrurhe, "The African Concept of Sacrifice: A Starting Point of Inculturation," *AFER* 40.4 (1998): 203-15.

Africans believe that the deities are their stronghold where they receive solutions to life's problems. If the deities are pleased, the society will be at ease. Therefore, they make every effort to maintain a smooth relationship with the spirit world. These spirits are consulted on life's issues to enhance peace, tranquility, and progress in the society.

Doug Priest Jr., agrees, offering a very simple and fascinating definition of sacrifice as the "Overcoming of the distance between God and man, the bringing of divine power to men, the restoration of wholeness to the community."[16]

Biblical Views of Sacrifice.

Jacob Milgrom argues that in the Bible, sacrifice is "a gift to the deity to induce his aid," and furthermore states that this seems to be the only definition that applies to all sacrificial systems. Furthermore, Milgrom stresses that under the Old Testament system sacrifice was a method for the Israelite to reach God, responding to the deep psychological, emotional, and religious needs of the people. This is one of the meanings of the Hebrew word for sacrifice. The word often translated "to sacrifice", *hiqrib*, comes from a verb meaning "to bring near," *qarab*. Therefore, a sacrifice in the Israelite tradition is the kind of offering that enables a person or group to approach God. Furthermore, he emphasizes that, sacrifice is the transference of property from the common to the sacred realm, thus making it a gift for God. As a gift, the sacrifice is sometimes intended to solicit divine aid. It can be (1) an external aid to secure fertility or victory or blessing, or (2) an internal aid to ward off or forgive sin and impurity or for expiation. Both meanings, for example, are ensconced in the burnt and cereal offerings (Lev 1 and 2). They are gifts to God in order to obtain blessing or forgiveness. Moreover, Milgrom concludes, the system underlying the sacrifices provides insight into the human need to feel personally connected to God

---

[16]Doug Priest Jr., *Doing Theology with the Maasai*, (Pasadena, Cal.: William Carey Library, 1990), 19.

and spiritually fulfilled.[17] If the Bible views sacrifice as a connection of human needs to God, then let us look at some theories formulated around sacrifice.

Theories of Sacrifice

Bernhard Lang has said, "If the Bible could elucidate African practices and institutions, why could not African society illuminate biblical studies?"[18] The fact that "religion is the relationship between the supernatural or deity and human being within his or her environment"[19] should not be overlooked all over the world. Sacrifice has been an element used to establish, maintain, or restore a right relationship between humans and the sacred order. Sacrifice is as old as religion because it appears in the early development of human populations.

According to Adolf E. Jensen, myths and rituals are produced from attempts to think about, and act with respect to, the meaning and value of their lives. People are "seized" by the "mystery of life" and are compelled thereby to think and act accordingly. In other words, they receive a "sacred vision" that permits understanding, and that would be "expressed" in myths and rituals (thoughts and actions).[20] These views about sacrifice have generated a great deal of literature on the subject of sacrifice. The next section deals with some of the literature used in this study.

Literature Review

In all established societies, religion is one of the important institutional structures that make up the total system. Humanity's social life is filled with different institutions of which religion is one. In the communion and communication between humans and God, sacrifice (or rituals more generally) plays a major role.

---

[17] Jacob Milgrom, *Leviticus 1-16*. (AB 3; New York: Doubleday, 1991), 440-41; idem, *Leviticus a Book of Ritual and Ethics: A Continental Commentary,* (Minneapolis: Fortress, 2004), 17.
[18] Bernhard Lang, *Anthropological Approaches to the Old Testament,* (Philadelphia: Fortress Press, 1985), 7.
[19] Robert Wuthnow, "Religious Orientations," 4.2382.
[20] Adolf E. Jensen, "From Myth and Cult among Primitive Peoples," *Understanding Religious Sacrifice: A Reader* (Ed. Jeffrey Carter; London: Continuum, 2003), 175-176, accessed 3 April 2013, EBSCOHOST e-book.

Both the Israelites and Africans, especially the Asante, consult God through prayer, sacrifice, and expressions of trust. Mbiti notes that, "Sacrifices, offerings and prayers are made, either directly to God or through the intermediaries of living-dead and spiritual agents." [21]

Sacrifice cuts across all the major religions of the world. For example, in the Ugaritic society, sacrifice was firmly represented as a means of receiving blessing. When King Kirta was troubled because his eight brothers and his seven wives died, he wept sorely, and then he was advised to make a sacrifice. He was to go to the mountain and to raise up his hands and sacrifice to Bull El his father, as well as to Baal and Dagon. When he came down from the top of the mount, he shared food with the people of the city.[22] Similarly in the Mesopotamian society offerings and sacrifices were apparent and wide spread. Expiatory sacrifice was part of the sacrificial system of Mesopotamian worship.[23]

Research Methodology

Rolf Rendtorf[24] appreciates the new approach that Mary Douglas brings into the study of the Old Testament especially with the respect to the structure of the Book of Leviticus.[25] He agrees that Leviticus can be read as a separate book since the readers of the book in the earlier times read it as a separate book.[26] Even though he agrees that it can be read as a separate book, he argues that it is still part of the Pentateuch. He shows this by explaining how Leviticus connects with the other books of the Pentateuch. He explains that God asked that the sanctuary be built in Exodus, but it is in Leviticus that what should be done in

---

[21] J.S. Mbiti, *African Religions and Philosophy,* (Nairobi: Heinemann, 1969), 180.
[22] Simon B. Parker, ed., *Ugaritic Narrative Poetry*: SBL writings from the Ancient World Series, (Atlanta: Scholars Press, 1997), 14.
[23] Stephanie Dalley, *Myths from Mesopotamia: Creation, The Flood, Gilgamesh, and Others*, (Oxford: Oxford University Press, 1989), 327.
[24] Rolf Rendtorff. "Is It Possible To Read Leviticus As A Separate Book? *Reading Leviticus with Mary Douglas* (ed. John F.A. Sawyer, (Sheffield: Sheffield Academic Press, 1996), 23-35.
[25] Mary Douglas, *The Forbidden Animals in Leviticus*, JSOT 59 (1993), 3-23.
[26] Ibid. 23.

the sanctuary is revealed: "Leviticus contains a very specific collection of texts, describing the rules and the meaning of the cultic proceedings at the sanctuary on Sinai, in particular the sacrifices."[27]

Mary Douglas is an anthropologist known for her writings on human culture, symbolism, and the interpretation of Leviticus. Drawing on her field work in many countries, mostly in Africa, she claims that Leviticus is not alone among religions regarding the role of a priesthood, but is a powerful intellectual statement about a religion that emphasizes God's justice and compassion. Among other things she spells out the forbidden items of the sacrificial victim. They are the fat called the *hard suet* (found around the kidneys and intestines), the *caudate lobe* (a long lobe sticking up like a thumb or a tail on the liver), and the *pair of kidneys* (Lev 3:15). All of these are to be burned on the altar.[28] Douglas argues that sacrifice is not an inhumane attitude towards animals, but is a transformation of the animal from one level of existence to another. Douglas argues that God loves all animals and that the sacrifice of animals is a way to preserve the lives of animals. For this God chose only domesticated animals for sacrifice.[29]

Jacob Milgrom is a prominent *Torah* commentator whose work focuses mostly on the book of Leviticus. Milgrom is concerned about how Christian scholars, and some Jewish scholars, regard the contents of the book of Leviticus as archaic. He says, "Ask a Jewish scholar to interpret a verse in Leviticus; he or she will pinpoint where it occurs in the Talmud, and what are its *halakic* (legal) implications."[30] Milgrom discusses the qualifications of the few animals that were chosen to be offered for sacrifice. He says, they "must chew the cud and show split hoof (Lev 11:3) . . . they effectively eliminate the entire animal kingdom from human consumption, except for the three domestic herbivores: cattle, sheep and goats."[31]

---

[27] Ibid. 26.
[28] Douglas, *Leviticus as Literature*, 73.
[29] Ibid. 74.
[30] Jacob Milgrom, *Leviticus:* xii.
[31] Ibid.

Peter K. Sarpong, a Roman Catholic Bishop of Kumasi, strongly believes in "inculturation"[32] and emphasizes that incarnating the gospel in Asante terms derives from a positive approach to the gospel and culture. He has worked extensively on Asante's nubility rites, in which the Asante perform a cleansing ceremony for a girl who is being introduced into the adult society. The Asante nubility rite ceremony involves "certain reparation rituals to cleanse the soul, *kra*."[33] He argues how the Asante embrace the reparation as a means for cleansing to ease their relationship with the ancestors and the gods. He also emphasizes that, as for the victim for the reparation sacrifice in Asante religion, sheep take the prominence, even though chickens are frequently used for religious purposes as the favorite victim for sacrifices to non-human spirits. He says, "Gods often require chickens to be offered to them in return for their assistance to men." Sarpong also agrees that sexual sin and sin in speech, especially the swearing of an oath, demands killing a sheep before the offender is tried. He explains some of the symbolism in the Asante tradition. For example, white symbolizes purity, virtue, joy, and victory. Sarpong stresses the importance the Asante give to sacredness in the spiritual realm and that the Asante believe that the underworld is inhabited by the ancestral spirits which are also sacred. Therefore, a dead body must be cleansed from the impurities of the world before it is bid farewell.

K. A. Busia, philosopher, economist, social anthropologist, and politician who became a prime minister in Ghana, observes the prominence of the chief or king's position in the life of the community and its religious worship. He says, "Only the chief could bring all the lineage together and sacrifice to his royal ancestors on behalf of the community as a whole … Before they

---

[32] J. Healey Sybertz, D., *Towards an African Narrative Theology,* (New York: Orbis Books, 1996), 26. *Inculturation:* the process of incarnating the good news in a particular cultural context…, a process by which people of a particular culture become able to live, express, celebrate, formulate and communicate their Christian faith and their experience of the Paschal Mystery in terms…that make the most sense and best convey life and truth in their social and cultural environment.

[33] Peter Sarpong, *Girls' Nubility Rites In Ashanti,* (Accra-Tema: Ghana Publishing Corporation, 1977), 61.

came together to settle in a town as a community the chief first sacrificed on their behalf."[34]   Only the king or chief has the right to do so. He offers sacrifice to cleanse the land before they settle on it because he believes that, something might have happened to contaminate the land before their arrival on the land. So before they settle down with their gods, reparation sacrifice must be offered by the king or chief. Busia works hard to describe those sins that are religiously committed and thereby required a cleansing offering.[35] He presents some case studies in which defilement had occurred in some way which demanded a reparation sacrifice. He also demonstrates that there are two Asante religious ceremonies called *Adae* of which one is celebrated on a Sunday, and the other on Wednesday. The *Adae* is celebrated when the spirits of the departed rulers of the clan are appeased, their names and their deeds are recalled, and their favors and mercy are solicited. The Sunday *Adae* is known as *Adae Kese*: this is the great *Adae* which is always held every six weeks on Sunday. The Wednesday *Adae* is the little *Adae*, celebrated every six weeks on a Wednesday.

Frank Kwesi Adams, a well-known scholar in the African Baptist Fellowship, explores the nature of the *Odwira Festival,* one of the Asante festivals for the cleansing of the community before ushering them into a new year. It contains a cleansing sacrifice to make the community whole before their ancestors. Adams examines the Odwira ideology and its implications for the understanding of the Asante self-identity. He also shows how some elements of faith seen in the Odwira festival could provide a framework for Christianity to engage Asante culture at a greater depth. He notes that "The Odwira was an occasion where the *kra* (soul) of the Asante was cleansed and baptized"[36] and then continues by saying, "These religious ideas and values, which have survived as positive features in Asante society, serve as a clue to

---

[34] Busia, *The Position of the Chief in the Modern Political System of Ashanti*, 36.
[35] Ibid. 70-72, 150.
[36] Frank Kwesi Adams, *Odwira and the Gospel: A Study of the Asante Odwira Festival and Its Significance for Christianity in Ghana* (Oxford: Regnum, 2010), 33.

Christian theologians who would like to develop theology starting with themes that are recurrent in African life and traditional religion."[37] Adams takes the history of the *Odwira festival* from the pre-colonial period to the post-colonial period. He demonstrates that the *Odwira* is a festival which the Asante celebrate to cleanse the ancestral stools and the entire Asante kingdom. The festival is an occasion where the spirit of individual is cleansed from the contamination of the world. The process of cleansing begins with the defilement of the totem of the group, and then its purification follows by pouring libations with prayers to ancestral spirits, and finally the eating of new yam to bring renewal and prosperity in the coming year. The meal is a ritual, a memorial, a sacrifice, and a fellowship. The *Odwira* festival is seen as an event where the past, present and future are united in Asante's cultural experiences, bringing continuity, sustainability and unity in Asante traditional religion.

The above scholars have exhibited their commitment to reveal the significance of *asham* sacrifice in different cultures and religions. This revelation encourages us to know more about the *asham* sacrifice. An important point that this comparative study reveals or confirms is that the conception of realities needing sacrifice is broader than the Western definition of "sin." Squeezing the Israelite texts into the Western conception does considerable injustice to them. The study also coincides with my personal knowledge and observations about some Asante religious activities which also conform to the results of personal interviews with some Asante chiefs who are the custodians of the Asante traditional religious heritage. We will now explore the *asham* sacrifice in Leviticus.

The Asham Sacrifice in Leviticus

The *asham* sacrifice is made to appease the sacred after it has cleansed or purged the stain of sin on the offender. Other cleansing sacrifices consist mainly of the sin offering (Lev 4), the Day of Atonement offering (the offering for the nation that atones for the sin of the priest and the people Lev 16), the offering of the Nazirite (Num 6), and the cleansing of a Leper (Lev 14:48-57).

---

[37] Ibid. 199.

Asham occurs when a sin has advanced to be accompanied by contamination or defilement. Milgrom agrees with this view when he says that Israel offers sin offerings to expiate desecration and offers *asham* or reparation offerings to expiate contamination. He continues by noting that sin brings defilement, but when the defilement is prolonged, it contaminates holy things, especially the sanctuary. He points out that the desecration of the sanctuary can go to the extent of desecrating the *sancta* which is God's personal name.[38]

In the Hebrew lexicon, the word *kiphar, atone* or "atonement"[39] has a range of possible translations such as cover, hide, wash away, rub off, obliteration of sin; the price of a life, ransom; cover over, pacify, and make propitiation. When the *asham reparation* is in question *kaphar* is followed by the preposition *min, from,* as in *mechattato, from his sin,* (Lev 4:26; 5:6, 10). The *asham, reparation* sacrifice is comprehensively discussed in Leviticus chapters 5, 6, and 7. It involves sin or *chattat* (5:1), and *asham* (5:2, 3, 4, 5), "atonement" or *kaphar* (5:6, 10, 13, 16, 18) "compensate"[40] or *shalem* (5:16). This sacrifice covers many branches of sins. The main branches are sin in utterance and in touching (Lev 5:1-4). It is in this sacrifice that we find the true mercy and great love of God for His children. Robin Routledge argues that the Israelites received their forgiveness from the sacrificial system, especially from the atonement. He stresses that the *atonement* is the key term for "cleansing or purification, or the payment of a ransom. He confirms that reparation, *asham* offering is one of the two offerings linked with making atonement.[41]

Leviticus 5 is open to all people, from the highest to the lowest person in the society. It contains the two types of expiatory sacrifices, the purification sacrifice (5:1-13) and a part of the *asham*, trespass, or reparation sacrifice (5:14-19), and the sin of violating sacred objects (which requires a twenty percent penalty; vv. 15-

---

[38] Jacob Milgrom, "Further on the Expiatory Sacrifices," *JBL* 115/3 (1996): 513-14.
[39] BDB. 497-99.
[40] BDB. 1022.
[41] Robin Routledge, "Prayer, Sacrifice and forgiveness," *EuroJTh* 18 (2009): 17-28, esp. 18.

16; cf Lev 22:14; Num 5:7).[42] The holy thing or sacred object could be any of the sacred implements or the sacred food in the sanctuary.[43]

Some scholars believe that the narrative of *asham* sacrifice in Leviticus begins in chapter 5:14. For instance, Sylvian Romerowski[44] understands the discussion to encompass Lev 4:1 – 5:13. I was not comfortable with Romerowski's arrangement at first because a careful examination of chapter 5 suggests that *asham* sacrifice begins at 5:1. I make this argument because at first, the chapter is dealing with the various defilements, and in verse 6, Yahweh says *vahevi et-ashmo,* meaning, "He shall bring his *asham* offering." This statement has created a lot of confusion among scholars on the subject of sacrifice in Israel. If one is not careful, one would think that part of the chapter identifies with the *asham* offering. However, I agree with Milgrom's argument that the section distinguishes between purification offering (Lev 4:1-5:13) and the *asham* or reparation offering (5:14-6:7). Milgrom's formula has attracted a lot of scholars. Martin Noth had earlier argued that verse 6 only consists of an introductory sentence and an incomplete formula. He continues that in verse 6 we note that the first appearance of the word *asham* really bears the sense of atonement for wrongdoing or penance. Yet the term is not a sacrificial term for "*asham* offering" for the sacrifices in 5:1-13 are always expressly characterized as "sin offering."[45] Initially, it is hard to accept this fact, but Leviticus 12 justifies this point by stressing that a nursing mother (v.1) who performs her purification offering for sin must bring a lamb for a burnt offering, and a young pigeon, or a turtledove, for a sin offering, to the door of the tabernacle of the congregation, to the priest (12:6), and if she is not able to provide a lamb, then she should bring two turtledoves or pigeons (12:8), just as it is stated in Leviticus 5:6-12. This is the sacrifice that Jesus' mother offered when Jesus was born; Mary offered two turtledoves or pigeons (Luke 2:24).

---

[42] Milgrom, "*Leviticus 1-16"* 294
[43] Sylvain Romerowski, "Old Testament Sacrifices and Reconciliation," *EuroJTh* 16 (2006):13-24.
[44] Ibid.
[45] Martin Noth, *Leviticus: A Commentary,* (Philadelphia: Westminster Press, 1972), 45.

In Lev 5:14-26, in regard to sin, wittingly or unwittingly, against the holy things of God the *asham* offering is a reparation offering that is offered for the forgiveness of the offerer, and the proper relationship is restored with God. A violation against the holy things of God, or against neighbor's property requires restitution to be made of one-fifth or 20 percent value of the item(s) added to its original value. According to Samuel E. Balentine, offenders had to bring an unblemished ram "convertible into silver by the sanctuary shekel," and must add one-fifth of its value as a penalty payment.[46] This requires that the ram must have a certain value which was not determined by human assessment but by the standards of the sanctuary. The offerer must add a penalty payment equal to 20 percent of the value of what has been violated. The penalty payment serves as part of the economic system designed to fund the temple. The restitution penalty safeguards against the temptation to appropriate, free of cost, the holy things of God as if they are simply an interest-free loan to be used for whatever purpose one chooses.[47] Milgrom shows that an *ephah* is estimated as equivalent to 22.8 liters of which one-tenth, would amount to 2.3 liters.[48] Milgrom calls this sacrifice, the *asham reparation* offering, a title that is accepted by other scholars, although the English Bible refers to it as *asham* or *trespass* offering.[49] The holy thing could be any of the sacred implements or the sacred food in the sanctuary.

According to Romerowski, an instance of this occurs when a tithe or something due to the sanctuary has not been brought, when some sacred food has been eaten by someone other than priests, or when a Nazirite vow had been interrupted, and such like. These are unintentional sins.[50] Milgrom also adds that the holy things are confined to the tabernacle *sancta* which refers to the entire tabernacle complex, and may include the cultic furniture, anything about and for the priests; even their land surrounding the Temple (Ezek. 45:3; 48:12,18) is holy and belongs to

---

[46] Samuel E. Balentine, *Leviticus Interpretation: A Bible Commentary for Teaching and Preaching*, (Louisville: John Knox Press, 2002), 47,48.
[47] Ibid.
[48] Milgrom, "Leviticus 1-16," *The Anchor Bible*, 398.
[49] Ibid. 319.
[50] Romerowski, 21.

God. The ornaments, dress, as well as the monies and animals for the Temple services are included.[51] Also, an offering must be made when a non-priest enters the sanctuary, as in the case of Uzziah, who offered incense in the sanctuary which he was not authorized to enter (2 Chron. 26:16-18).[52] The offence(s) against the holy things of Yahweh go an extra mile to require an extra object with the victim for sacrifice. The ram is for atonement for the sin committed unintentionally, and the monetary value of the item is for the replacement of the affected item (vv. 15, 16).

Another example of asham sacrifice is found in Lev 6:1-7. In this case, someone keeps his or her item with another person, and the keeper lies about what has been kept in his or her safe-keeping, or someone lies about a pledge made, or commits robbery or extortion from a neighbor. In this case also, the value of the item and a fifth part of the regular value of the item plus a ram without blemish for atonement shall be brought to the priest.

In Lev 7:1-8, the *asham* sacrifice is explained. The animal is killed where the burnt offering is killed, and blood is sprinkled all around on the altar. All the fat that is the fat tail and the fat that covers the entrails, the two kidneys and their fat, and the fatty lobe attached to the liver above the kidneys are removed, and the priest burns them all on the altar of Yahweh. In Lev 14:12, 24, 25, a trespass sacrifice is made on behalf of a person who has been cleansed from his or her leprosy. Lastly, in Lev 19:20-22, if a man has sexual intercourse with a female slave who is engaged to another man, and if her freedom was never bought or given to her, they should not be put to death. The man will only pay a fine because she is a slave. He must bring a ram for his asham offering to Yahweh at the entrance to the tent of meeting. In Yahweh's presence, the priest will use them to make peace with Yahweh for this sin. The man will be forgiven for this sin.

Now that we have had enough, for now, about the asham sacrifice in Leviticus, we shall move to the asham sacrifice in Asante in the next section.

---

[51] Milgrom, "*Leviticus 1-16*," 320-323.
[52] Ibid. 346.

Asham Sacrifice in Asante

Asham sacrifice falls under cleansing sacrifices. According to Deji Ayegboyin, it is a sacrifice which is offered when a worshipper violates a prohibition. He gives an example from among the Akans (of which Asante is part). If a man indulges in sexual intercourse in the bush, it is believed that the two people have defiled themselves and that their defilement has affected the Earth goddess; therefore, she must be appeased. On such occasions, the sacrifice should be offered at the sacred grove to appease the Earth mother and ancestors. [53]

Many offences in Asante call for *asham* sacrifice. K. A. Busia[54] and Peter Sarpong[55] show the classes of offences which require the *asham* sacrifice. When a person fails to control his or her tongue or language for instance, the reproduction organ of humans must be mentioned by first saying, *Sebeoo*, meaning "Excuse me please!" when the person is in the presence of a member of a royal house. If one infringes this rule, one has caused defilement to the royal and the land; therefore, a sheep has to be slaughtered as a sacrifice. When a person swears an oath, which is not supposed to be sworn, for example, the oath of a king or a chief which no one is allowed to swear except a rightful royal, the person will be compelled to kill a sheep for sacrifice before he or she is tried. If someone accidentally kills a person, or if a person commits suicide, or causes a serious injury to self, a sheep must be sacrificed to the ancestors in order to purge the misfortune. If there is incest, or an adulterous congress with a chief's wife, the male offender must bring a sheep for sacrifice to appease the ancestors and the gods. Likewise, if one transgresses against a chief, for instance, by "blessing" (cursing) him, the oblation of a sheep to the ancestors is very necessary. Busia shows that the offences of which the chief takes cognizance are religious offences. The list of those offences was drawn up by the Confederacy Council of Asante at 1946. These are offences by which native courts must demand the slaughter of sheep because they are religious and therefore cause defilement to the land.

---

[53] Ayegboyin, 2:583.
[54] Busia, 70-72.
[55] Sarpong, *Girl's Nubility Rites*, 60-72.

Organization of the Study

The study has five chapters. Chapter one is the introduction of the study. It covers the central research problem and objectives, methodology, the conceptual framework, Literature Review. The chapter will define sacrifice from various approaches and some theories on sacrifice. It will review different literature on the topic and describe the research methodology in chapter one. In the research method section, the study has included sources from scholars who have worked on the topic of this study as well as other related works. Also, personal interviews were conducted with some traditional chiefs in Asante. However, the study does not quote any of them directly because what they said agrees with the scholarship used and the author's personal understanding and observation of the Asante religion at the various cultural centers.

Chapter 2 of the study focuses on *asham* sacrifice in Israel. Starting from the background of Israelite sacrifice, this chapter gives a brief explanation on each of the five main sacrifices of the Israelites as stipulated in Leviticus. After the brief discussion on five sacrifices, the chapter dwells mainly on *asham* offering and shows how it is performed, as well as the types of objects used in the *asham* sacrifice. The chapter also explains the meaning of *asham* sacrifice in the Israelite context, and the relationship that the *asham* sacrifice holds between Yahweh and His people.

Chapter 3 continues in the same manner focusing on *asham* sacrifice in Asante. It discusses the overview of Asante sacrifice briefly, and dwells mainly on *asham* sacrifice and how it is performed. The chapter shows the types of objects required for the *asham* sacrifice and brings out the meaning of *asham* sacrifice in the Asante religion and the position of God in the sacrifice.

Chapter 4 compares *asham* sacrifice between the two religions. It compares the place of worship, the priests, the object(s) for sacrifice, and how the sacrifice is performed in each of the religions. It shows where the two religions are similar and also reveals their differences. Chapter 4 is the concluding part of the study in which I try to help the reader make his or her own decision on the proceedings of the study. Also, the reader must note that chapter 4 is the place where I have begun the process of constructive theological work.

Conclusion

The two religions we are studying believe in the existence of a deity who is holy and sacred, but the Israelite religion recognized only one God called Yahweh while the Asante religion believes in many deities such as the Supreme God, ancestors and lesser gods. The two religions offer sacrifice to receive blessing and forgiveness of sin from the deities of each. Thus if Christianity talks about sin or draws an Asante toward the idea of sin and purification, this idea will not be strange or foreign to an Asante man or woman.

Chapter 2: Asham Sacrifice in Israel

This chapter discusses the *asham* sacrifice of the Israelites in Leviticus chapters 5-7, 14, and 19. There is the need to clarify the fact that the *asham* sacrifice in Israel is a two-edged sword that cuts both left and right as it functions in the society and at the same time functions in the religious sphere. This chapter will show what *asham* is, the different types of *asham* in Leviticus, and the religious functions of the *asham*. I will then discuss the *asham* offering that is offered when (a) a person has desecrated the holy things of Yahweh in ignorance (5:14-19), (b) when a person defrauds his or her neighbor (6:1-7), (c) when a person with a skin disease is cleansed and brought back into the community (14:12, 24, 25), and (d) when a person lies with a betrothed slave girl (19:20-22). At the end of the discussion, the reader will understand that the *asham* sacrifice is offered to appease Yahweh which brings about the reparation of the relationship between humans and Yahweh. Also, the reader will understand that the *asham* sacrifice[56] appears in several forms.

The root *ashem* can often mean "to be, feel blameworthy." According to Anderson, the *asham* is often linked to verbs meaning "be paid" *shlem hashav*. Also, the *asham* can be converted into a monetary equivalent and simply paid.[57] Although Eugene Carpenter and Michael Grisanti agree with Anderson, they explain the term *asham* as to become self-reproached, incur self-condemnation, bear the responsibility for some offense, culpableness, stand under a curse, involve judgment, bear iniquity, and be offered in a state of culpableness. The word group includes "*asham* (*āšām*) reparation offering," and the accompanying noun *ashem* (*āšēm*) "culpable under judgment," *ashma* (*'ašmâ*) regret, blame, reparation offering," and shame, object of blame.[58] Looking at the words "pay," "incur," "bear," "stand under," and "be in state of" may seem to make *asham* much like a burden that one

---

[56] *Asham* sacrifice is used to differentiate the "incurred guilt," from the "sacrifice" for guilt offence.
[57] Gary Anderson, "Sacrifices and Offerings (OT)," *The Anchor Bible Dictionary,* 5.880.
[58] Eugene Carpenter and Michael A. Grisanti, "870 *asham*", *New International Dictionary of the Old Testament Theology and Exegesis.* 1.553.

has put upon oneself that must be removed before one can be relieved of the guilt. However, one should not overemphasize this aspect of the definition.

Milgrom refers to *asham* as "reparation offering". This term "reparation offering" or "*asham* sacrifice" will be used interchangeably throughout this study. A reparation offering is present when a sacrilege has taken place. According to Milgrom, "sacrilege" is the legal term for the wrong that is redressed by the reparation offering. The opposite word to sacrilege is "sanctify" as in "you committed sacrilege against me . . . you did not sanctify me" (Deut 32:51).[59] In other words, the *asham* repairs the properties that belong to Yahweh and humans. It also repairs or restores a broken relationship between Yahweh and humans, as well as between human and human. The reparation offering serves as *asham* for situations in which property belonging to Yahweh or to another human being has been misappropriated and therefore must be restored with a twenty percent (one-fifth) penalty before a reparation offering is performed.

There is, therefore, much for *asham* to accomplish in the Israelite religious life. It does not stand for reparation only. It primarily compensates for a sin against Yahweh. In this regard Milgrom explains that the denominator of all instances of sacrilege is sin against Yahweh. Sacrilege involves sin against Yahweh and none other, for there are other offenses that are committed in some way but do not require an *asham*. For example, stealing a neighbor's money or article is a trespass, but since it does not involve Yahweh as a witness by swearing an oath in His name to bind the contract or agreement, an *asham* is not required, instead a double payment of the affected item or money is required (Exod 22: 7-9). Thus it is clearer and more understandable when Milgrom emphasizes that the *asham* responds to sin against God.

Averbeck continues the discussion by noting that Israelite references to the Philistines (1Sam 6:1-8), as well as texts from other ancient Near Eastern cultures show that the concept was not limited to the Israelite religion. He argues that a so-called *asham* offering pericope begins when a person commits a violation and

---

[59] Milgrom, *Leviticus*, 51.

sins unintentionally in regard to any of Yahweh's holy things (Lev 5:15a).[60] He confirms that Milgrom is right with regard to the overall purpose of the *asham* offering: it is designed "to make atonement for" desecration of "*sancta*," that is mishandling of holy (sacred) things by treating them as if they were common rather than holy (Lev 22:10-13).[61] Averbeck's assertion that the concept of the *asham* offering for the desecration of *sancta* was not limited to Israelite religion but was certainly known elsewhere in the ancient Near East (1 Sam 6:3, 4, 8, 17)[62] is true in Asante religion as well. For instance, the African, especially the Asante, also believes that some of the causes of sickness occur as a result of provoking the spirit realm to anger. Luc de Heusch shares this view and says:

> One common function of African sacrificial rites is to restore the normal physical condition of man - his health, or his status – which has been compromised by offence contrary to the Christians' link of sacrifice to sin, which is a metaphysical impurity resulting from the transgression of a major prohibition. The African believes that the ill-health condition is as a result of making the gods or ancestors angry – which is a transgression as sin.[63]

The good relationship between the profane and the sacred results in good health regarding the profaned. Ephraim Donkor confirms Luc's view that human sin brings about ill-health and says:

> This love is predicated upon the fact that God abhors evil (Nyame mmpe bone). So, to lead an unethical life is to alienate oneself from God resulting in misfortunes and death, because the righteousness of God is based on the fact that he abhors injustice, which God duly recompenses (*Nyame betua woka*). The notion of divine retribution is

---

[60] Ibid. 559.
[61] Averbeck, *asham,* 1:559.
[62] Averbeck, "Sacrifices and Offerings," 720.
[63] Luc de Heusch, *Sacrifice in Africa: Structural Approach,* (Bloomington: Indiana University Press, 1985), 5.

etched in Akan social consciousness because an individual suffering unjustly would invoke the divine retribution "God will recompense."[64]

The Israelites knew and believed that Yahweh is a "healer" and that His agents were also empowered to heal. They also believed that Yahweh causes sickness to people while, healing is perceived as the work of Yahweh and His Divinely empowered agents. In the Old Testament writings of the Bible, especially the Pentateuch, the Prophets, and the Writings, Yahweh is seen as a healer.[65] For example, Abraham prayed to God to heal the house of Abimelech from the punishment of the sickness of infertility that had befallen him and his people (Gen. 20:17). In Exodus 15, Yahweh sent a disease upon Egypt. Yahweh Himself claims the appellation of a "healer" and says, "There is no other God beside me, I kill and make alive, I wound and I heal" (Deut. 32:39), and "I am Yahweh your healer" (Exod. 15:22).

The people in Old Testament times, especially the Israelites, believed that Yahweh used the plague of disease as part of His disciplinary and correctional measures (cf. Job 5:17-18). Other places in the Old Testament where Yahweh is seen as a healer include for example Ps 30:2; 41:4. Moreover, the healing of Yahweh sometimes comes with forgiveness (Ps 103:3) which indicates that Yahweh is the cause of some diseases to some people or a group of people like a family and the society as well. Also, Yahweh's healing comes with deliverance from imminent destruction (Ps 107:19-20), and accompanies the renewal of the human spirit (Ps. 147:30). This type of destruction could only be curbed by the *asham* sacrifice.

The Israelite tradition believed that Yahweh controlled all human life; therefore, He does whatever He wishes to (Deut 30:15 19-20). In Israel, the belief that disease contaminates life and threatens the communion with God and humankind was very prominent. According to Johnston, "It deals with disease as a contamination of this life and a threat to communion with

---

[64] Anthony Ephraim-Donkor, *African Spirituality,* (Lanham, Maryland: University Press of America, 2011). 64.
[65] Meir Lubetski, "Medicine and Healing," *The Anchor Bible Dictionary*, 4.659.

God."[66] This point justifies the need for the *asham* sacrifice to be performed to appease Yahweh and to purge the contamination of the disease. The *asham* sacrifice causes the healing to take place before the performance of the sacrificial ritual. The Israelites believed that some of the diseases that happened in their lives were the result of divine judgment. Johnston notes that "Most widespread diseases recorded in Pentateuchal narrative are interpreted as divine judgment, notably the various plagues in Egypt, and in the wilderness."[67] Examples are also noted in the following passages: Num 12:10; Lev 26:16; Deut 28:21, 27-28, 35.

Other Religious Aims of the *Asham* Guilt Offering

Furthermore, Knight observes regarding the *asham* offering that the Law of Moses is not a mere "dry as dust" legal code. Rather, it concerns itself with an individual's personal relationship with God and rejoices when a person repents and desires to return to fellowship with the Yahweh.[68] This is so because Yahweh takes sin seriously to the extent that there is no petty sin in His presence. A later text puts it thus: "Therefore do not suppose that it would be a petty sin if we were to eat defiling food; to transgress the law in matters either small or great is of equal seriousness, for in either case the law is equally despised."[69] A similar view appears throughout the Hebrew Bible. The cleansing and healing nature of *asham* prepares the way for all the other sacrifices in Israel because when Yahweh is angry with humans because of their sins his relationship with them is broken. The *asham* sacrifice, therefore has to be introduced to restore the relationship so that other sacrifices will be accepted by Yahweh. A typical example is seen at the cleansing of a person with a skin disease. In Lev 14 after the priest had completed the eight days rituals (Lev 14:1-11) the priest then offered an *asham* offering before the other sacrifices could follow as in Lev 14:11-31.

---

[66] P.S. Johnston, "Life, Disease, Death," *Dictionary of the Old Testament: Pentateuch.* 533.
[67] Ibid.
[68] George A. F. Knight, *Leviticus,* (Philadelphia: The Westminster Press, 1981), 45.
[69] 4 Maccabees 5:19.

Knight explains that as against the other rituals which we have now observed, this *asham* takes precedence over all other sacrifices and is the first to be offered up during the ritual of the eighth day.[70] What Knight says, to my understanding, is that one cannot restore friendship when the action of showing remorse expressed in *asham* is not put forward. For example, when one was settling a case between two people, the process would reach a point where the one who offended the other must surface his fault before the other. But that need not make the offended appeased until the offender has taken an action to prove that he or she is truly sorry. This is what Knight points out what the *asham* offering does. It is the action that someone who has sinned against Yahweh takes to appease Him, and then Yahweh could begin the restoration of fellowship with the offender. We should note however that Knight did not say that the *asham* precedes all the other sacrifices at every occasion.

The Objects for the *Asham* Offering

The animals required for sacrifices had certain qualities laid down by Yahweh. They were to meet certain standards. Thus the animal offered in sacrifice for the *asham* offering had to reach the same required standard. In this regard only one animal was prescribed by Yahweh for the *asham* offering, a ram from the flock, one without defect and of proper value in silver. The value is standardized by way of the sanctuary shekel (5:15, 18; 6:6; 19:22). Also, there needed to be some restitution regarding the loss plus an additional twenty percent of the value of what the person has failed to do in regard to the holy things (5:16), or the item of a neighbor that is affected (6:4-6).

The Various Occasions for the *Asham*

The reparation *asham* appear in several forms in Lev 5:14-19; 6:1-7; 14: 12, 24, 25; 19:20-22. They occur under the following circumstances: (a) when a person has desecrated the holy things of Yahweh in ignorance (5:14-19), (b) when a person defrauds his or her neighbor (6:1-7), (c) when a person with a skin disease is cleansed and brought back into the community (14:12, 24, 25),

---

[70] Knight, 23.

and (d) when a person lies with a betrothed slave girl (19:20-22). We will consider each situation in turn.

When someone trespasses and desecrates the Holy Things of Yahweh in ignorance (5:14-19) according to Milgrom, "The two categories are: (1) the sacrilege against sacred space, and (2) the violation of the sacred oath."[71] He notes that when a sacred oath is broken, the violated *sanctum* is none other than the Deity Himself. Yahweh's name, by which an oath is taken, is called a *sanctum*, God's holy name. Sacrilege against a deity is considered a serious offense in all the religions of the world. The Asante and Africans in general believe that epidemics and natural disasters, even droughts, are caused by the anger of the gods and the ancestors; therefore, sacrifice must be made to appease the gods. In some cases, the severity of the offence could be reduced when the offender feels he or she has done wrong and confesses. But in the offence where Yahweh's name or belongings are contaminated, as I see it, the confession itself does not remove the offence. This detail explains why confession is not mentioned in this case. What is seen here is that the offender receives forgiveness only when he or she makes the required *asham* sacrifice.

Milgrom gives an example where the Hittites believed that their god (storm god) could send plague to the people because,

> They have violated their sanctums, and they have broken their treaty oath. The Hittite gods punish not only the offender but also his or her household. Israel and the neighbors of the ancient Near East believed that sacrilege against sanctums threatened the general welfare. Every un-apprehend act of sacrilege against God, whether against the sanctums or against the name of god, leads to the destruction of the community as well as the offender. Israelites believed that sins against God are not punishable by any human, and collective punishment is a divine right.[72]

Milgrom pictures the condition which one goes through when confronting the issues of *asham*. He explains that it is a picture of a person who is experiencing psychological (and perhaps even

---

[71] Milgrom, *Leviticus,* 51.
[72] Ibid. 52-54.

physical) suffering whose cause he or she does not understand. Because the one suffering cannot attribute his or her suffering to any sin they have committed, he or she attributes it to an unwitting offense against God, confirming the psychological truth that one who does not know the exact cause of his suffering imagines the worst. Milgrom continues by explaining that this section speaks to the unwitting sinners who without knowing what sin they have committed to cause such grief believe they affronted the deity, committed sacrilege against the *sanctums*, and incurred liability to Yahweh (v.19). *Asham* is provided for the individual as a way to repair the unknown wrong and, it is hoped, thereby to ease his or her suffering.[73] Through the *asham* Yahweh provides an answer for a person in torment because of a wrong conscience committed or suspected to be in error.

However, Gane adds that sacrilege includes violation of an oath (e.g. Ezek 17:18-20) where one misuses Yahweh's holy name (Lev 19:12; cf 20:3; Ezek 36:20-22). Thus the *asham* sacrifice does not address only unwitting errors. Sacrilege is a grave offense that carries severe penalties, as shown by the stoning of Achan for misappropriating property destined by the Lord for destruction (Josh 7), and the national exile that resulted from King Zedekiah's violation of an oath (Ezek 17:18-21; 2 Kgs 24:20; cf. 2 Kgs 17:3-5). Gane proceeds furthermore, arguing that there are two kinds of cases associated with committing sacrilege (5:14-6:1-2). The first concerns the misuse of property belonging to Yahweh (5:14-19), and the second has to do with the misuse of human property through the misuse of Yahweh's name in an oath (6:1-7).[74]

On the misuse of Yahweh's property, Gane elucidates two subcases: (1) an inadvertent misuse of which the sinner later becomes aware (vv. 14-16), and (2) an inadvertent misuse of which he or she remains unaware (vv. 17-19). Gane says that, in the first case (5:14-16), just as Milgrom has pointed out, the Israelite violates the boundary of holiness by inadvertently misappropriat-

---

[73] Milgrom, *Leviticus*, 55.
[74] Roy Gane, *Leviticus, Numbers: The NIV Application Commentary*, Grand Rapids: Zondervan, 2004, 133.

ing something that belongs to Yahweh for his or her own purpose. One example of this inadvertent misappropriation is to eat produce that has been dedicated as a tithe or first-fruits. Such misuse must be committed inadvertently (v. 15) in order to be expiable by sacrifice. This implies that the same offense committed deliberately would have no sacrificial remedy, as in the New Testament account of Ananias and Sapphira. According to Gane, Yahweh killed them because they deliberately withheld something they had dedicated to Him (Acts 5:1-11).

Before the *asham* reparation offering is performed, the offender must pay the misappropriated amount plus a twenty- percent penalty to Yahweh through the priest. The seriousness of sacrilege required a ram "the most valuable animal ever required of a commoner"[75] (cf 4:23, the law for the chieftain). The offerer has the option of paying the value of the ram to the sanctuary in silver by the kind of shekel that is the standard there (5:15; 6:6).[76] It can be deduced from this point that the sanctuary has its own weights by which the priests determined the value of the ram. It is difficult to state whether the priests could be cheated by the offender when bringing the item(s) because once there is a measuring device to determine the weight, cheating would be minimized. The offender has to replace what had been misappropriated and supplement it with an amount equal to one-fifth of the value of the misappropriated holy things. When these are given to the priest, he would perform the expiatory ritual with the ram, and the person would be forgiven.

In the second subcase (vv. 17-19), the sin is an inadvertent violation of any of the Lord's prohibitive commandments ("Thou shalt not"). It is different from that in chapter 4 where the offender finds out what he or she has done wrong (4:13-14, 22-23, 27-28), but in 5:17-19 an *asham* is required even though the sin is not disclosed to the sinner. The unknowing individual may have a kind of negative experience that causes him or her to suspect a violation.[77] This negative experience could be suspected based on what was going on in one's life that is contrary to his or her

---

[75] Ibid.
[76] Ibid. See convertibility of value into shekel in Leviticus 27.
[77] Ibid. 134.

expectations. W. H. Bellinger emphasizes the involuntary nature of a violation against the holy things of the Lord: "The involuntary nature of the breach is emphasized in verses 17-18 ... even though he does not know it and the wrong he has committed unintentionally."[78]

In Leviticus 5 in the English translation, the first type of defilement involves the violation of the holy things of Yahweh because when one commits any of the offences, he or she is contaminated, and if nothing is done about it before he or she has contact with anything belonging to Yahweh, those things would be defiled as well. Milgrom calls this sacrifice the reparation offering[79] because when an offence is committed, the affected person or the thing loses value, and the lost value must be repaired, replaced, or restored. The holy thing could be any of the sacred implements or the sacred food in the sanctuary. According to Romerowski, an instance of this occurs when a tithe or something due to the sanctuary had not been brought, or when some sacred food had been eaten by someone other than priests, or when a Nazirite vow had been interrupted and the like. These are unintentional faults.[80] Milgrom also adds that the holy things were confined to the tabernacle *sancta*, everything pertaining to the entire tabernacle complex, including the cultic furniture, anything about and for the priests, even their land surrounding the Temple (Ezek 45:3; 48:12, 18) as well as the ornaments, dress, monies, and animals for the Temple services.[81] The offence(s) against the holy things of Yahweh require an extra object with the victim for sacrifice. The ram is for atonement for the sin committed unintentionally, and the money of the item is for the replacement of the affected item vv. 15, 16. When this sin is committed, a ram without blemish as well as a restitution of the thing desecrated and one-fifth part of it are brought to the priest.

---

[78] W. H. Bellinger, *New International Biblical Commentary Leviticus, Numbers,* Peabody: Hendrickson Publishers, Inc., 2001, 43.
[79] Milgrom, *"Leviticus 1-16,"* 319.
[80] Romerowski, "Old Testament Sacrifices and Reconciliation," 21.
[81] Milgrom, "Leviticus 1-16," 320-323.

The *asham* offering in Israel was legally accepted. Averbeck shows how it works in the community. He explains that the restoration plus a fine of one-fifth referred to the priest in Lev 5:16 corresponds to a regular legal pattern in Israel (Num 5:5-10). The restitution made it possible for the offender to make atonement and receive forgiveness from Yahweh (Lev 15:15, 16).[82] One important thing that must be taken into consideration in 5:17-19 is the phrase: "If a person sins, and commits any of the things which are forbidden to be done by the commandments of Yahweh" (5:17). In this case, when a person violates God's commandments not only in regard to holy things but also in relation to any area of life and comes to feel that he or she might have done something that God forbids and begins to feel responsible for it, then the offering of an *asham* brings about forgiveness. The real point in this case is that the sacrifice of the *asham* assumes no restitution or restoration except for the addition of twenty percent of the value of the defiled life. How could one replace a defiled life or give one-fifth of one's life to a priest? The point is that Yahweh wants repentance and forgiveness. Therefore, the offender has to survive purely by the grace of Yahweh, which is extended upon the completion of the *asham* sacrificial ritual.

When a Person Defrauds the Other Regarding Something Deposited, for Robbery, Extortion, and Lost and Found (6:1-7)

Another case of *asham* sacrifice is found in Lev 6:1-7. In this case someone has kept his or her item with another person, and the keeper has lied about what has been kept in his or her safekeeping, or someone lying about a pledge made, or robbery or extortion from a neighbor. In this case also, the value of the item and a fifth part of the regular value of the item plus a ram without blemish shall be brought to the priest for atonement.

On this issue Milgrom says the unwitting violations were very significant because people believed that as long as the sacred is not infringed, the gods would not molest them. The unwitting violation of Yahweh's commands requires expiation for *sanctum*

---

[82] Averbeck, "Sacrifices and Offerings," 721.

desecration.[83] Milgrom notes that when a person engages in fraud with respect to a deposit, theft of investments, or withholding another person's property, the person commits sacrilege against Yahweh. Here, restitution is the first thing to do; only after the rectification has been made with one's fellow can it be sought with God (cf. Matt 5:23-24). If someone finds a lost object and swears falsely about any economic transaction or feels culpable and wishes to return something gained fraudulently, then this *asham* sacrifice becomes relevant.

In other words, the situation where a person acts inappropriately towards a fellow human being in regard to a broken promise is also a breach of faith against Yahweh because he or she has sworn in Yahweh's name (possibly in the presence of the congregation of Israel, or at least before witnesses).[84] Therefore, to break such a promise is to violate the sacred and to break faith with Yahweh. For example, people may lie about property that has been entrusted to them and claim that the entrusted property is his or her own. Also, a thief or fraudster may claim that the item that he or she has stolen or defrauded belongs to him or her (6:2). Again, a person who has found a missing item can claim ownership of the item (6:3). In all these cases the offender swears falsely before the Lord. Anyone culpable of such must make the *asham* offering. The offender also restores to the offended party whatever he or she misappropriated (6:4-5), with an additional twenty-percent of the value of the property, a ram without any defect and of the proper value for the *asham* ritual (6:6). Only then would the offender be considered forgiven (6:7). It can be seen here, although not found in the text, that the *asham* offering stands as substitutionary atonement where the ram is put to death instead of the offender or the culpable person. Although other sacrifices may include the idea of substitution, the reparation sacrifice is offered to compensate God for the loss He has suffered as a result of sin.

When a person feels that he or she may be culpable of a sin, he or she should go to the priests and once the priest finds that the person's act is an encroachment upon the divine sphere, he or she

---

[83] Milgrom, *Leviticus,* 56.
[84] Ibid. 56-58.

must expiate by sacrifice. The priests in Israel, among other things, worked to offer sacrifices in the holy place, and at the same time received God's message, and made cultic enquiries for the people. They pronounced divine blessing upon the people (Num 6:22-27; Deut 10:8), mostly on public occasions (Lev 9:22). The priest pronounced oracles announcing the will of God for certain decisions. Sometimes they used the Urim and Thummim, a divine device to judge matters. As Exod 28:30 puts it, "And you shall put in the breastplate of judgment the Urim and Thummim, and they shall be over Aaron's heart when he goes in before Yahweh. So Aaron shall bear the judgment of the children of Israel over his heart before Yahweh continually"; cf. Num 27:21; Deut 33:8; Ezra 2:59-63. The priest had no power to change the rule else they have arrogated to themselves the power to alter Yahweh's decree.

Similarly, Gane thinks that misusing human property along with misusing the name of Yahweh is a deliberate sin because it involves unfaithfulness to the Lord's commands and deceiving one's neighbor with lying and swearing falsely. He stresses that "such ethical wrong against other persons would simply be handled by the civil courts (cf. e.g. Exod 22:1-15), but through swearing falsely, thereby misusing God's holy name to defraud contains elements of sacrilege."[85] The underlying factor of the *asham* of defrauding one's neighbor is deception through unfaithful oath-taking in the name of Yahweh. Bellinger supports the idea that this type of violation goes beyond a case that the civil courts could handle because of its complexity: "Violations indicated here are difficult to prove because they often involve conflicting testimony. [*He also emphasizes the significance of restitution and reparation in this situation, saying,*] Restitution and reparation probably entail an act of repentance and confession."[86] Obviously, the defrauding of one's neighbor by oath in the name of Yahweh involves *asham*. Here, the *asham* sacrifice is required because an oath is always taken before a witness or witnesses, so the evidence is clear. It goes beyond a case that the civil courts

---

[85] Gane, 134.
[86] Bellinger, 44.

could handle because with the *sanctum* attached to the act of deception, it becomes a religious offence rather than a civil case. As the study proceeds, we shall look at the *asham* sacrifice that ushers a cleansed person from a skin disease back into the community.

The Cleansing of a Leper or Person Suffering from a Skin Disease, and Return to the Community (14:12, 24, 25).

In Lev 14:12, 24, 25, we read of the *asham* sacrifice required of a person who has been cleansed from his or her leprosy. Here, Averbeck stresses that the *asham* sacrifice is the ritual procedure for the cleansing of the leper (Lev 14:1-20), and that "leprosy" refers to any skin infections. Knight supports Averbeck's claim for the healing efficacy of the *asham* sacrifice as a cleansing power for the leper. He stresses that the *asham* is performed before Yahweh (vv. 12, 16) and at Yahweh's command (v. 1):

> Moreover, because the action is of God, it is bound to be effective, therefore, he shall be clean (v. 20). The *asham* is effective even for the poorest of the poor. It is always a lamb that is slain to conclude the ritual"[87]

Averbeck refers to Exodus 24:5-8 to support the understanding that by this ritual Israel was transformed into "a kingdom of priests and a holy nation."[88] Knight adds that "The leper's, *asham*, moreover, is the only sacrifice in Leviticus to include the wave offering. This places it on a high pedestal of importance."[89]

Each item in the cleansing process plays a particular role as Willis claims. The association of the living bird with fresh ("living") water and red materials (cedar and scarlet yarn) points to the association between blood and life and death. The blood of the bird and the "death" of leprosy are linked, and the living bird and the water symbolize how life "carries away death." The leper is moving from the state of uncleanness to cleanness, just as the priest was transformed from a common priest to one consecrated for the task of offering sacrifices. As Willis puts it, "The completion of the process on the eighth day also marks a person's

---

[87] Knight, 23.
[88] Averbeck, *asham*, *NIDOTTE*, 1:563.
[89] Knight, 23.

migration across symbolic boundaries, in this case from the realm of death to the realm of life."[90] According to Gane:

> Before slaughtering the lamb, the officiating priest presents it and a log (smallest biblical unit for measuring capacity) of oil and elevates them as an elevation offering *tenuphah* to formally dedicate them to the Lord, and slaughters the victim. The application of some of the blood on the right extremities of the offerer who is undergoing purification: lobe of the right ear, thumb of the right hand, and the big toe of the right foot as prescribed in (7:2) is the same as the consecration of the priests in (8:23-24). The consecration completes when oil is applied on the right extremities of the offerer on top of the blood, and the rest of the oil is poured on the head of the offerer.[91]

Erhard S. Gerstenberger contributes to this discussion by beginning with a question:

> Why must a guilt offering be presented after convalescence and for the sake of cultic rehabilitation of the recovered person? It is not that thanksgiving has been forgotten in Leviticus but because people in antiquity believed that a close connection was obtained between known and unknown transgressions on the one hand, and a particular illness on the other. Both Job's friends and Jesus' contemporaries view illness as God's punishment, and certain skin diseases are especially taken to be a "stroke" delivered by God for the sake of marking guilty persons for their sins.[92]

In support of his argument, Gerstenberger gives an example of King Uzziah who presumed to carry out sacrificial acts (2 Chron 26:16-21). He had a skin disease until the day of his death, and because he had the skin disease he dwelt in a separate house (v. 21). Gerstenberger says "Miriam's skin disease case in (Num

---

[90] Timothy Willis, *Abingdon Old Testament Commentary: Leviticus* (Nashville: Abingdon Press, 2009), *129*-130.
[91] Gane, 247-248.
[92] Erhard S. Gerstenberger, *Leviticus A Commentary,* (Louisville, London: Westminster John Knox Press, 1996), 179.

12:9-15) is clear evidence of God's punishment on those who sin."[93] Here, Gerstenberger's question is useful and significant, even though he has partly answered the question regarding the *asham* sacrifice not being required for thanksgiving, yet we should understand that the cultic rehabilitation is necessary in order to restore a healthy skin. In other words, it is for the healing of the skin disease because the people believed that known and unknown sin could have connection with skin disease as punishment from God. As an example of this, during the exodus of the Israelites, Yahweh sent skin disease on the Egyptians when they disobeyed the commands of Yahweh (Exod 9:8-12).

Also, the *asham* does not stand for culpability alone. It also functions when someone stands under a curse, and the skin disease is believed to be a curse from God. The *asham* sacrifice is deployed for those under judgment in some way, thus it is necessary for the contamination of the curse on the person to be purged and cleansed. If he or she is not cleansed or purged from the contamination, this disease could be contagious, and could desecrate the community as well as the holy things of Yahweh when he or she took part in the worship of Yahweh. The job of *asham* then, was to purge and cleanse, hence the need for the performance of the *asham* sacrifice after the disease has been healed. Miriam was shut outside the camp seven days because of her skin disease (Num 12:14, 15) according to the law concerning skin disease "But if the priest examines it, and indeed there are no white hairs in it, and it is not deeper than the skin, but has faded, then the priest shall isolate him seven days" (Lev 13:21; 14:8).

The last point of consideration in this chapter is the rape case of a slave girl.

When Someone Lies with a Slave Girl Who Has Been Betrothed (19:20-22)

Lastly, in Leviticus 19:20-22, if a man has sexual intercourse with a female slave who is engaged to another man, and her freedom was never bought or given to her, both the man and the woman should not be put to death, but the man will only pay a fine because the woman is a slave. He must bring a ram for his

---

[93] Ibid. 182.

asham offering to Yahweh at the entrance to the Tent of Meeting. In Yahweh's presence, the priest will use them to make peace with Yahweh for this sin, and the man will be forgiven for this sin.

Milgrom confirms that:
> In Israel adultery was considered as a violation of the Sinaitic covenant but where investigation shows that the betrothed slave had not been emancipated, her paramour or seducer could not be punished. He is not an adulterer because she is not a legal person. Nevertheless, he has offended God by desecrating the Sinaitic oath and must bring his sacrificial expiation.[94]

Milgrom elaborates further that had she been free, she would have been subject to the laws governing a betrothed woman, which in all codes, biblical and non-biblical alike, prescribe death for her and her paramour (e.g., Deut 22:23-27). "They shall not be put to death because she has not been freed" implies that if her infidelity took place after her manumission, her paramour and she would have been put to death.)

On the other hand, had she remained a slave and had not been betrothed to another, then the question of the death penalty would not have arisen at all. Instead, since a slave is considered chattel in all the law codes of the ancient Near East, her owner (slave master) should have been awarded damages. In this case, the Bible does not compensate the owner at all. Because she is betrothed, the master is in effect only her partial owner and therefore not entitled to compensation. On the other hand, because she still is a slave, the laws of adultery are not applicable, and their penalties cannot be imposed on her paramour. Milgrom says, "The matter here is not dealing with law, but teaching that whoever wishes to be holy must beware of fornicating with a slave girl. It is given because it is a reparation offering prescribed for cases of מעל (*ma'al*) (Lev 5:14-26) desecrating (or unfaithfulness to) the name of Yahweh."[95]

---

[94] Milgrom, *Leviticus,* 238.
[95] Jacob Milgrom, *Leviticus 17-22,* (AB 4; New York: Doubleday, 1991), 1665.

Milgrom comments on the expression, "they shall not be put to death," which he thinks means that whereas all cases of fornication with a married woman constitute a capital crime, in this case if judicial examination proves that the woman is technically still a slave, the death penalty cannot be imposed. In such cases the priests also served as judicial judges in Israel. According to Duke, the priests in Israel were assigned to handle religious cases.[96]

The *asham* differs from all other sacrifices in that the required animal may be commutable into money according to the value fixed by the sanctuary (Lev 5:15, 18, 28). This explains why the *asham* is brought to the priest and not to the entrance of the Tent of Meeting, which would imply that the offerer involves presenting an animal (Lev 5:6). According to Milgrom the death penalty is not applicable because "the betrothed woman is still a slave, *asham* is required because the betrothal was solemnized by an oath, and its violation through adultery would therefore constitute *ma'al*, a crime against God that under mitigating circumstances is expiable by *asham*.[97]

Aaron Rothkoff agrees with the view above on the case of the betrothed slave girl and emphasizes that:

> Seduction of a betrothed slave girl (Lev 19:20-22), was a violation of property right and the offender in any case must confess his sin and make full restitution with a fine of one-fifth of the damage and offer a guilt offering. If the offended party is not alive, then his kinsman could receive, and if there was no one then the payment went to the priest (Num 5:5-10).[98]

---

[96] The judges in Israel started from the heads of households to recognized elders of status to appointed officials" (Gen; Exod 18:5-27; Deut 1:9-18; there judges in each town Deut 17:8-13; 19; 16-17; 21:1-5). The priests special line in the judiciary was at where the case lacks witnesses, or there were conflicting witness, "it appears that in difficult cases which involves a lack of witnesses or conflicting witnesses, the priests stood as divine representatives and perhaps were expected to divine the truth as they did in case of the wife suspected of adultery (Num 5:11-31) R. K. Duke, "Priests, Priesthood," in *Dictionary of the Old Testament: Pentateuch.* 653.
[97] Milgrom, *Leviticus 17-22*, 1671-1673.
[98] Aaron Rothkoff, "Sacrifice," *Encyclopedia Judaica.* 17.640.

This asham procedure illustrates that one cannot commit such sins of adultery with impunity; there must be a payback. When Yahweh gave the Ten Commandments, a man's wife was considered to be part of his belongings (Exod 20:17).

Summary

To summarize the discussion so far, the *asham* denotes culpability incurred, or when a person is in a state of being culpable or standing under a curse or judgment, as well as the liability incurred overall. The *asham* responds to a sin against Yahweh. The *asham* involves a payment for an impacted sacred item of God, or for a neighbor who has been defrauded after the name of God has been used to bind an agreement between two parties in an oath. It is a sacrifice that is presented when a person commits an act of sacrilege. In short, the *asham* works as a repairer and restorer of a desecrated item that belongs to God or humans and at the same time restores the relationship between God and humans, as well as the relationship between a person and his or her neighbor. This sacrifice cleanses and purges sin and brings forgiveness of sin to humans. Again, the *asham* possesses a healing potency whereby the punishment of disease might have emanated from the anger of God upon a person or a group of people but was avertedand the healing of a wrong under certain circumstance is restored. The healing nature of sacrifices such as the *asham* was and is recognized among some major societies of the world such as Israel, ancient Near East, and Africa.

Although the *chattat* sacrifice and the *asham* sacrifice seem to be similar, they are similar in the offence that is unintentional and the offender feels a sense of culpability. The *asham* is caused by a breach of faith against Yahweh which is crossing the boundary that separates objects that belong to Yahweh from profane objects (5:14, 15). This type of offence demands restitution where reparation or damages are to be paid. The material or victim for the *asham* offering is a ram without any defect valued in silver shekels according to the sanctuary shekels (5:15).

Conclusion

To conclude, this study has focused so far on the *asham* or reparation offering in Leviticus. The chapter has shown that *asham* is necessary when one becomes culpable, or stands under a curse, or culpability under judgment, or a liability incurred, or a sacrilege against God, and a desecration of the *sanctum* (the holy name of God). It has shown that when *asham* takes place, it requires a reparation offering, or *asham reparation sacrifice*. The *asham* offering is necessary for purging the desecration of the holy things of Yahweh, beginning with His name and including the items in relationship with His worship. The sacrificial victim is a ram with no defect, and must be accompanied by restitution plus twenty percent of the value of the item harmed. Another aspect of the *asham* offering is sin against the Temple and its items (holy things) of Yahweh. Also, when a person defrauds a neighbor, the cleansing of a person with a skin disease, and the humbling of a betrothed slave by another man demand a reparation with a ram and one-fifth or twenty percent of the value of the item desecrated. The reparation sacrifice is offered to repair the broken relationship between humankind and Yahweh. Yahweh is merciful and kind towards humans and wants a strong relationship, so humankind ought to recognize and embrace the blessing.

   I conclude that the acceptable *asham* sacrifice must be a domesticated animal (particularly a ram) without blemish or physical defect owned by the offerer. The offerer brings the animal to the entrance of the Tent of Meeting or the Temple. The offerer hands all the sacrificial items such as the ram, the restitution of the item affected by contamination or defrauding plus the twenty percent to the priest, and the priest manages the items as Yahweh has prescribed.

   We learn from the reparation offering that people must respect the boundary that separates objects that belong to God from those that belong to humans, and the boundary that separates those objects that belong to other people from those that belong to oneself.

   It is clearly seen that the *asham* sacrifice plays a significant role in the lives of the Israelites, both in the spheres of religion and society to bring forgiveness, and life, and to establish good relationship between God and humans. This sacrifice acts as a symbol of Christ's sacrifice on the cross for mankind. Sin is universal and permeates all the major societies of the world. Apart from fulfilling religious purposes within the Israelite context such as calming or restraining Yahweh's anger caused by some offense, atonement (Lev 10:17; Deut 21:8-9), cleansing or removing sin, effecting reconciliation, and consecrating and bringing forgiveness to the sinner,[99] the *asham* works beyond the religious sphere to accomplish its ultimate function in the society as well. As Gerald A. Klingbell emphasizes:

> A ritual is never an isolated event, executed in a clean room atmosphere … It happens and is enacted in a concrete historical context and in a particular cultural and religious milieu … ritual pragmatics tries to describe the illocutionary force of a given ritual or sub-rite and seeks to locate it in the larger societal context.[100]

Therefore, if the children of Yahweh pay proper attention to the asham sacrifice and its purpose, the world will claim its meaning of existence. The next chapter will deal with the *asham* sacrifice in the Asante religion, and society.

---

[99] Glenn D. Pemberton, "Leviticus," in *The Transforming Word.* 170.
[100] Gerald A. Klingbell, *Bridging the Gap: Ritual and Ritual Texts in the Bible*, (Winona Lake: Eisenbrauns, 2007), 205.

Chapter 3: Asham Sacrifice in Asante Traditional Religion.

The main focus of this chapter is on the *asham* sacrifice in Asante religion. In collecting data for this chapter, I will use my personal experience on the subject in question as an Asante indigene. Also, reference to literary works on Asante history and politics are employed. Furthermore, other sources of information include personal interviews with some Asante chiefs who are the custodians of the Asante religious and cultural activities, a visit to the Asante cultural centers, watching films on Asante cultural programs, and observations of some cultural activities in Asante. Before we get to the issue of *asham* sacrifice in the Asante religion, which is the main topic of this chapter, we shall look at some of the elements of the Asante religion. The elements include concepts such as Supreme Being, Sacredness or Holiness, Temples, Shrines, Altars, Priesthood, Sacrifice, Prayer, Victim of Asham sacrifice, and other type of sacrifices in the Asante traditional religion. On the main topic, the chapter will provide a list of some Asante religious sins, and some case studies of some of these sins.

The Asante are very protective of their beliefs in the Supreme Being, the spiritual realm, and their relationship with these sacred entities (God, spirits, and ancestors) to the extent that when the Europeans came to the coastal areas of Ghana and established their religion, it took them many years before they could penetrate into the Asante land. It was not that the Asante hated the Europeans, but they were strongly protective of their religion lest they lose it. As Evans notes:

> The coastal tribes in Ghana have long been familiar with Europeans – Portuguese, Dutch, Danish, and English – at their fortified trading-posts and exposed to foreign influences; but the Ashanti avoided, until comparatively recently, all contact with the white man except in clash of battle, and the strength and order of the Ashanti kingdom tended to preserve ancient custom and tradition from adulteration.[101]

---

[101] John T. Evans, "Akan Doctrine of God" in *African Ideas of God; A Symposium* (Edwin W. Smith; London: Edinburgh House Press, 1961), 241.

Bernhard Lang observed regarding this tendency of the Asante, "If the Bible could elucidate African practices and institutions, why could not African society illuminate biblical studies?"[102]

I remember growing up; as a child I grew up in a Christian home. My parents were Christians and I attended a Christian mission school. We were taught at school by the Christian missionaries to understand that our traditional religion was against the will of God. In this regard Godfrey N. Brown observes:

> Finally, pervading the whole social structure of Asante, there was the Golden Stool,[103] the soul of the people, brought down from the heavens by a miracle. Truly the Asante Confederacy was unique. It was not surprising, though it was tragic, that expatriates from Victorian British failed to understand it and represented it as the stronghold of Satan.[104]

On one hand, some aspects of the traditional religion are unwelcoming to Christian spiritual growth. Yet on the other, some ideas and values of the Asante religion illuminate the idea that God made all human beings and the universe.

It is obvious that the Asante religious ideas and values have certain relationships with some biblical values. This is why the purpose of the study to examine the similarities and the dissimilarities of asham sacrifice in the Israelite and Asante religions is significant. We should not overlook the fact that, "religion is the relationship between the supernatural or deity and human being within his or her environment."[105] Throughout the ages and all over the world, sacrifice has been an element used to establish,

---

[102] Lang, 7.

[103] According to Sarpong, it is a kind of seat or chair purely gold; it is supposed to have been brought down from heaven by the great priest of Asante, Okomfo Anokye. It is the object of deep veneration in Asante. It is held to be more important than the king of Asante and the King of Asante is referred to as the "One who sits on the Golden Stool." The king derives his kingly powers from this unique stool. *Ancestral Stool Veneration in Asante*, (Kumasi, Ghana: Goodshepherd Publishers Ltd., 2011), 10.

[104] Godfrey N. Brown, *Africa in the Nineteenth and the Twentieth Centuries: A Handbook for Teachers and Students*, (Ibadan, Nigeria: Ibadan University Press, 1966), 246.

[105] Wuthnow, 4: 2382.

maintain, or restore a right relationship of humans and the sacred order.

Thus the Asante rely on sacrifice as a means of getting in touch with the spirit world to enhance good relationships. Grillo expresses the dependability of sacrifice in the African religion.

> Blood sacrifice is the archetypal model. In African religions, blood sacrifice shows life's dependence on death and establishes the reciprocal bond between spiritual and mortal realms. In African religions the life force released through blood sacrifice "feeds" the gods and the 'living dead' (ancestors) even as it channels their animating energy to the human community. A devotee must not forget the ritual duties that sustain this relationship; divinities and ancestors while supportive are also demanding and can trouble a negligent supplicant by causing illness or chronic misfortune.[106]

Unlike the Israelite sacrifices where Yahweh has prescribed some parts of the animal and other items that are not to be used in sacrifice, the Asante sacrifice has no such forbidden items. But the Asante have taboos and totems. The principal forbidden item for sacrifice in Asante religion could not be a part of an animal prescribed but rather a whole animal(s) that is forbidden. Sarpong, writing from an Asante perspective, views taboo as "Any infringement of a forbidden act is a criminal offence as it is held to imperil the society."[107] For example, it is forbidden for the *Asantehene*, the king of Asante's *ntoro* totem *bosommuru* (state sword),[108] to have contact with an ox, cow, domestic and wild dog, and monkey. Adams explains that "Its own register of avoidance and taboos are monkey, ox, cow, domestic dog, and wild dog, and its own totems are the python and mouse."[109]

The Asante believe that taboo is a societal problem which may be caused by an individual, but the society or the whole community will bear the consequences as Sarpong emphasizes:

---

[106] Laura S. Grillo, "African Rituals" in *The Wiley-Blackwell Companion to African Religions*. (Ed. Elias Kifon Bongmba; Oxford: Wiley-Blackwell, 2012), 122.
[107] Sarpong, *Ghana in Retrospect:* 53-55.
[108] (See appendix N.)
[109] Adams, 62.

> It is sufficient for one fool to commit fornication with a girl under the age of puberty and there is bound to be famine in the community unless something is done ritually to cleanse the community of the abomination. The spirits are punishing the community for the crime of an individual.[110]

Incest taboos apply to a larger range of people in Africa than in Europe. In many African societies, and the Asante in particular, the incest taboo does not only apply to members of the same family, but it also applies to members of the same clan or lineage. Taboos are the sins that can be classified as religious sins that require the *asham* sacrifice in the Asante religion. Sarpong confirms that people who commit this type of sin are required to pay a fine and also sacrifice a sheep to the ancestors:

> The latter category of sin is classified as taboos, and in the olden days the penalty for their disregard was death, a very heavy fine or perpetual banishment. As they were said to have estranged or threatened to estrange the ancestors or the gods from the community and so imperil its well-being, those who offended against these taboos were, in time past, tried by the king or chief, and their trial began with the sacrifice of sheep to the ancestors, the gods and the Supreme Being who were thought to have been infuriated.[111]

Totems are emblems of hereditary relationship to the people of the community. Animals and plants which had assisted the ancient founders of the nation might be called totems in the Asante religion. Ghanaians in general have the same concept about totems, and Sarpong relates:

> A number of features are generally associated with totemism. In the first place it is a group institution, though the group may not be based on unilineal descent or (and this is the case of the Akan) localized. Lineages may respect lions, crocodiles, lizards, certain types of food etc., either because these creatures or items are thought to have

---

[110] Sarpong, *Ghana in Retrospect*, 53.
[111] Ibid. 54.

been the progenitors of the lineages or because they supposed to have helped the lineages in one way or other or to have mystically manifested themselves to some lineage member in the past.[112]

Among the Akan, the different clan names carry with them different totems. The Asante as one of the Akan tribes has different clans, and each clan claims different lineal descent, hence different totems. For example, the Asante tribes have the following clans: the Aduana clan whose totem is a dog; the Agona clan has the parrot; the Oyoko clan has the falcon as totem; the Bretuo clan has the leopard as its totem; the Asona clan has the crow or boar as its totem; the Asenie clan has the bat as its totem; and the Ekuona clan has the buffalo as its totem, while Asakyiri clan's totem could not be identified by this study. All these eight clans are different groups of people in the Asante tribe, and in each Akan tribe, these clans are found with the same symbols or totems. Perhaps, at some point in history these animals probably did something to endear themselves to the people of a particular clan. The animals that are regarded as totems are ritually avoided by the clan. These totem animals may not be eaten by any clan member. Levi-Strauss explains that "If one eats one's totem even unwittingly, one will be troubled by boils or suffer in some other way, and will not be relieved until one is ritually cleansed."[113] This definition of totemism in the African context may not however be the same as in other societies around the world. Claude Levi-Strauss presents a broader view of this phenomenon from different societies. He gives an example:

> In Tikopia the animal is conceived neither as an emblem, nor as an ancestor, nor as a relative. The respect and the prohibitions connected with certain animals are explained, in a complex fashion, by the triad of ideas that the group is descended from an ancestor that the god is incarnated in an animal, and that in mythical times there existed a relation of alliance between ancestor and god. The

---

[112] Ibid. 59.
[113] Sarpong, *Ghana in Retrospect,* 60.

respect observed toward the animal is thus accorded to it indirectly.[114]

Also, the prohibitions attached to the eating of a totemic animal in Asante is different from that of the Taumako clan. Levi-Strauss explains, "The pigeon which is closely connected with Taumako clan is not eaten, but there are no scruples against killing it because it plunders the gardens. Moreover, the prohibition is restricted to the first-born."[115] According to Levi-Strauss, totemism has been a topic that has aroused the interest of many scholars. "Totemism has already taxed the wisdom and the ingenuity of many scholars, and there are reasons to believe that it will continue to do so for many years."[116] Although according to Peter Sarpong, the Asante connect totems as "symbols for spirit in relation to groups or clans,"[117] there are some societies which have clans without totemic names. Levi-Strauss notes "the Crow, Hidtsa, Gros-Ventre, and Apache have clans without totemic names, and Aranda have totemic groups which are distinct from their clans."[118] Many societies have the idea of totemism as an expression of human relationship to natural species such as animals, plants, and objects.

The next section will deal with concepts in the Asante traditional religions that are related to this study, including Supreme Being, sacredness and holiness, temples, and altars, priesthood, sacrifice, prayer and other types of sacrifices in the Asante traditional religion.

The Concept of a Supreme Being

Just as the Israelites believed in a supreme being, so too do the Asante. The Asante also believe that this Supreme Being appeared to them on Saturday, so He is called *Kwame*, and they believe that He controls the universe. According to Mbiti, the Akan (of which Asante is one of the tribes) consider God to be the ruler of the sky, earth, and underworld. The Asante say that God has still the power to change this order, and they believe that having

---

[114] Claude Levi-Strauss, *Totemism*, (Boston: Beacon Press, 1963), 29.
[115] Ibid. 28.
[116] Ibid. 4.
[117] Sarpong, *Ghana in Retrospect*, 62.
[118] Levi-Strauss, 5.

created all things, God made provision of sanctions for laws and customs. The Asante claim that, "God created things in an ordered fashion, and that he created an orderly and harmonious world where everyone could perform his own duties."[119] The Asante, even though their religion is not that of a book, have many things such as the name, rituals, and other things that show there is a Supreme Being who owns the universe. Evans has argued that:

> The Asante knew God before Christians came to Asante land; they have different names to call unto the Supreme Being...the Asante did not borrow the concept of a Supreme Being. But the Asante believe that God is omnipresent and he is seen or visible in his works which is why one cannot search and find an image or representation of God in any shape or form. Asante believe that the nature of God is spiritual which is why they have the proverb that, *wope aka asem be akyere Onyankopon (God) a, ka kyere mframa,* which means, "If you want to tell God anything, tell it to the wind." For us to get information about the Asante idea of God, we need to carefully examine the name or names they use for the Supreme Being and the praises they give to Him. The common name for the Supreme Being in Asante *Onyame (God)*. The Asante say that this word *Onyame* comes from two words, *nya* "to get" and *mee* "to be full" which means if you possess Him, you are satisfied. *Onyame* is regarded as a God of Fullness, a God of Satisfaction.
>
> There is another derivation *Onyankopon,* Onyame – koro – pon (Onyame the One – the Great). Another name is *Twereduampon,* the Great Tree you can lean against without falling. There is another derivation that connotes "full of grace or mercy" *Odomankoma.* Some of the praise names are *Bore-bore or Oboade:* The Creator; *Totorobonsu or Amosu*: The giver of rain; *Amoawia*: The giver of sunshine; *Nana*: Grandfather; *Otumfo*: Mighty;

---

[119] John S. Mbiti, *Concepts of God in Africa,* (London: S.P.C.K, 1970), 51,71

Daasebre: He who beyond all thanks; *Berekyirihunu*: All seeing; *Tetekwaframua*: Enduring from ancient time.[120]

In this passage, Evans is demonstrating that the Asante people believed in the existence of the Supreme Being before the Europeans came to the Asante community with Christianity. Before the arrival of the Europeans, the Asante had known that the Supreme Being is the creator of the universe and that He lives forever. These beliefs could be identified through the names and praises they refer to the Supreme Being in their local language as shown in the passage.

Molefi Kete Asante and Emeka Nwadiora confirm that the Asante believe that God created the heavens and the earth. They believe God to be the Great Ancestor on whom they rely because when all things fail on earth, they turn to the God in heaven, but they could not identify the gender of the God of heaven. This implies that God has revealed Himself through creation to His creatures. In that case, all people all over the world should be ready for God's business:

> The Asante believe that God is the Great ancestor ... The Asante fear God because when everything fails on earth, they appeal to God . . . The Asante believe in one great God and are politically monarchical but have no regular worship . . . The gender of God is not identified by the Asante, and they believe that God is the god of rain . . . Nyankopon is the creator of all gods, and so many golden objects are symbolic of his radiance.[121]

The worship is not directed to God because the Asante believe that God must be worshipped through the ancestors and the lesser gods who are the intermediaries between God and humans as will be seen later in the discussion.

It is clear here that the Asante know and understand God in the various ways God has manifested Himself to them just as He showed Himself to the Israelites in various ways, and they gave him different names. The Asante consider the earth as "the great–

---

[120] Evans, 241-259.
[121] Molefi Kete Asante and Emeka Nwadiora, ed., *Spear Masters: An Introduction of African Religion,* (Lanham, Maryland: University Press of America, 2007), 1-10.

breasted goddess," who is second to God and for whom Thursday is observed as her day.[122] The Asante believe that God reveals Himself through heavenly and earthly things. The Asante thinks of himself or herself as mere nothing before God and looks for God's mercy. Sarpong notes that "Temples are not built for God, images of God are not displayed, but there are countless images of lesser gods in wood, clay, brass and stone. They believe that God is the last judge who does not vent His anger on one who commits a wrong inadvertently." [123]

The Asante do not believe and respect the supreme God alone. They also believe in other deities such as ancestors and lesser gods: "God comes into the limelight especially on the individual level, as opposed to the ancestors and lesser gods who come to the forefront in lineage and tribal worship respectively."[124] According to Sarpong the Asante worship other deities:

> Even though they are creatures of God and subordinate to Him, they may use their enormous powers independently of Him. They are distinct from the spirit of the dead and may be domiciled also in man-made shrines. But they seem to have a special love for those "residential areas" which induce fear and reverence. They demand worship and obedience from man, in default of which they inflict punishment on him . . . More importance is attached to deities of chiefdoms than to those whose influence extends over a village or lineage. They are said to have means of supplying the needs of their subjects . . . Sacrifices are made to them either to repay the benignity of the good ones or to avoid the malignity of the ill-disposed ones . . . some being domiciled in natural places and objects such as rivers, rocks, mountains, and the sea.[125]

Without any dispute this passage clearly shows that the Asante give the same honor and trust to the Supreme Being, that they

---

[122] Mbiti, *Concepts of God*, 115.
[123] Sarpong, *Ghana in Retrospect*, 12.
[124] Ibid, also Kwadwo Osei, *A Handbook on Asante Culture*, (Suame-Kumasi: O. Kwadwo Enterprise, 2002), 76.
[125] Sarpong, *Ghana in Retrospect*, 14-15.

give to the lesser gods. This point differs from that of the Israelites because Yahweh had instructed them not to give the honor due Him to anybody or anything else. This act in the Asante traditional religion places the intermediaries in equal position with the Supreme Being which Yahweh is jealous of and hates.

The Concept of Sacredness or Holiness

The Asante religion also recognizes that things pertaining to God, the ancestors, and the gods are sacred. The Asante regard some acts as committed against the sacred therefore demanding *asham* sacrifice. The Asante believe in sacredness, so when a chief is enthroned, he is looked upon as the ancestral spirit by the people: "From the moment that the chief is enstooled,[126] his person becomes sacred."[127] To illustrate how the Asante hold the sacredness of the chief and the stool in high esteem, Osei Kwadwo explains, "For example, in the olden days, when a woman was in her menstrual period, she was forbidden from visiting our stool

---

[126] When somebody from Southern Ghana is elevated to become a chief or king, the term used is: "He is going to be enstooled." The word "stool" is used to mean the carved wood on which a chief or queen mother sits. It is also used to denote the office of a chief. Stool land is used to denote the land which belongs to a stool which also means the stool's property. Stool house is used to mean a house built for the stool by the subjects and which is used by the occupant of the stool or which is hired to people and the money derived from the hiring used by the chief for the stool's activities. When the occupant of a stool dies, the term used is "The stool has fallen" (Akonnwa ato). (Kwadwo Osei, 137, 139). The enstoolment of an Asante chief or king happens in this way according to Kwadwo Osei and Peter Sarpong: "On this day the chief-elect would be flanked by his close relative or accompanied by a select few and goes into the stool house, where he finds the blackened stools of his predecessors. Upon the one belonging to the most renowned of the dead chiefs, he is lowered and raised three times. He has been brought into the closest possible contact with the ancestors and, therefore, is enstooled. He is now more than just a head of a state. He is in a sense an ancestor himself. From that moment everybody must call him Nana (Grandfather), and this irrespective of his own age and that of the person addressing him. He may be a young boy and the addresser an old man, yet by reason of his intimate contact with the blackened stool, he is the "grandfather" or the old man. He has become sacred, and he is treated accordingly with the greatness veneration.] Osei, *A Handbook*, 139; Sarpong, *Ancestral*, 18. See Appendix A-D.
[127] Sarpong, Girls' Nubility Rites, 60.

houses."[128] Likewise Sarpong notes, "Next to God are the ancestral spirits who play a very prominent role ... Like god the ancestors are treated with respect. The Asante pay so much attention to their ancestors that ... it was said that the religion of the Asante was mainly ancestor worship."[129]

The Asante pay due respect to the ancestors because before one becomes an ancestor, the person during his or her lifetime on earth, whether a chief or an elder, must have been a person who contributed greatly toward the development of the family or the community:

> To qualify to be immortalized by a black stool, one must have lived an exemplary life and have done a lot to enhance the image and the development of the community during one's lifetime. In his lifetime, an ancestor should have played his role in such manner that his life becomes an example and inspiration.[130]
>
> According to Emmanuel Asante, the leader (chief or king) becomes a link between the humans and the external world: The festivals point to the people's conception of the traditional ruler as an agent of modern development and the link between his community and the external world."[131]

The role of the chief or king of Asante involves various duties such as prayers, offerings, judging, law making, and others. Osei Kwadwo explains the role of the Asante king:

> He is a leader who tries to prevent calamities and deaths by "praying and offering drinks to God, the ancestors and the deities to avert calamities and guard the state ... he does this whenever he pours libation for the powers that be ... he also prays to God Almighty, the deities of the land and the ancestors for the forgiveness of the sins of the people. This he does by slaughtering rams to the

---

[128] Kwadwo Osei, *A Handbook*, 12.
[129] Sarpong, *Ancestral*, 146.
[130] Emmanuel Asante, "The Relationship between the Chieftaincy Institution and Christianity in Ghana," in *Chieftaincy in Ghana: Culture, Governance and Development*. (Ed. Irene K. Odotei and Albert K. Awedoba; Accra, Ghana: Sub-Saharan Publishers, 2006), 242.
[131] Emmanuel, *Asante*, 243.

deities and the ancestors on festive days. The chief is the war general of his people. He pledges to the people during his enstoolment that he would lead them in war. The chief also serves as the judge of his people. He settles conflicts among his people. His judgment is expected to be nothing less than the truth and just because he is guided by the spirits of the ancestors and the deities to give impartial judgment. As such he has the right to impose punishment to offenders. The chief and his elders make laws for the state and see to it that the laws are obeyed first by himself, his elders and then his subjects. If anybody contravenes the laws of the land, he deals with him according to the laws of the state. The chief sees that the customary rites of the state are respected. He initiates development projects for his state and leads his people in their implementation. He has the right to levy the people for the execution of projects and he has to render accounts to his people. The elders appointed by the people to help the chief in the administration of the state swear oath of allegiance to him before each of them takes office. The principal advisers of the chief are his elders, his wives, and the queen-mother.[132]

The passage above clarifies the role of the Asante king or chief as the representative of the deities (God, the ancestors, and the lesser gods) to the people on the earth. The king pours libation to these deities to appease them in order to avert a calamity or to request a blessing on the community. The king in turn is given the authority and right by the deities to manage the affairs of the community based on the principles laid down by the deities. The king can punish the wrong-doers and must see to the development of the community. Thus, the Asante worship God and the other spirits and lesser deities; the next section will show where these deities are worshipped.

---

[132] Kwadwo Osei, *An Outline of Asante History Part 2 Volume 1*, (Suame-Kumasi: O. Kwadwo Enterprise, 2000), 11.

The Concept of Temples, Shrines, and Altars

The Asante have temples and altars where their rituals are conducted. According to Mbiti, shrines may be private, family, public, or communal shrines. Some shrines are constructed in the form of small huts or mounds in homesteads or behind the houses. Some shrines are also located in groves, trees, rivers, and rocks. The shrines are believed to be the symbolic meeting-point between the heavens or sky and the earth, and therefore of the invisible and visible worlds. Mbiti explains:

> Shrines are used for rituals, ceremonies, sacrifices, and offerings, and praying. Shrines are regarded as sacred place therefore it is holy so it is not put for public use lest it be desecrated. There are keepers of these places. Altars are small structures on which sacrifices and offerings may be placed. They may be in temples, and in the open.[133]

Some shrines and altars belong to an individual; some belong to the community.

The cult of the Asante religion did not originate in the present Asante land. The religion had been with them since their migration from the northern part of West Africa. Today, most of the Asante shrines are imported from the northern part of Ghana.

Richard P. Webner observes:

> These are rival yet basically similar cults that originated in the north from quite widely separated parts of Ghana, Ivory Coast, and Burkina Faso. Having spread south, toward the coast, they established southern client shrines, and promoted regular pilgrimages to and from the north. Their growth resulted in the routinized dissemination of ritual beliefs and practices. Eventually, to a large extent, they were displaced in the south by a "revival" of quite different cults, all of which claim southern origins. But the direction of ritual importing was not reversed: none of the cults that had southern origins gave rise to client shrines in the north ... Shrines in the south, especially among the Ashanti and other Akan peoples, were derived

---

[133] John S. Mbiti, *Introduction of African Religion,* (New York: Praeger Publishers, 1975), 145-146.

from the north's widely separated central places, such as in Ghana.[134]

I agree with Webner because I have experienced many occasions where people are said to have been called by any of the lesser gods, and they were taken to the northern part of Ghana to train to become a priest or priestess simply because the source of the spiritual call is from the north. The Asante religion has a very strong arm of conversion. People adhere to the values and the ideas of the Asante religion. Some Christians still practice both Christianity and the Asante religion at the same time. Those who do so believe that the God of the Asante religion responds to requests (whether to bless or to punish) quickly once they give Him what He demands. For example, some people who live in the city may attend Christian church services and activities regularly, but when they go to their villages they participate in the practice of the traditional religion. They do this because some believe that they are serving the same God since the name of God is mentioned first in the Asante prayers. Also, others believe that the God of Christianity is too slow to act for their liking. Although the Asante religion wins souls, they do not convert people by open evangelism like the Christians or Muslims. Rather, they share their ritual beliefs and practices.

According to S. A. Thorpe:

> Primal religions in general have no Sacred written Scriptures, but are passed from generation to generation orally ... As a result, people in primal cultures do not engage in missionary activity. They do not attempt to convert people from other tribes or villages to their own religious ways of thinking or acting ... For much the same reason tolerance and flexibility are hallmarks of primal religions ... Even though people do not make an overt at-

---

[134] Richard P. Webner, *Ritual Passage Sacred Journey: The Process and Organization of Religious Movement*, (Washington: Smithsonian Institution Press, 1989), 225, 230.

tempt to convert others to their ways of thinking and acting, there is a great deal of spontaneous borrowing and exchange of ideas.[135]

People are converted into the Asante religion because of the way they live. For example, conversion takes place when someone sees the way someone else's business is booming, or a person may see a friend or colleague suffering from one thing or other and are directed to where the problem can be solved. In this case, if the colleague is successful, he or she also directs others to the same place. One way of conversion occurs when a person who was directed by a friend to a priest may not have the same problem as the friend, the priest may not have the solution, so the priest through his network can direct the person to the right priest who has the gift of solving such problems.

One thing that we must understand about the lesser gods and other spirits is that each of them specializes in one area of interest. Therefore, the priest who serves a specific god may be good in a certain aspect of problem solution. However, in order for the priest or priestess to be more powerful, and to be able to solve many different problems of life, he or she must have been trained, or connected with other priests. One experience I had in Nigeria was when a traditional priest visits a colleague priest, in their conversation one would ask the other, "do you know how to solve this problem?" When the other says no, the one who has knowledge about the solution would teach the other colleague.

Mbiti adds to the discussion of temples and shrines by observing; "The Akan and Ashanti have altars in their homesteads at which they make offerings of food, especially eggs and wine."[136] Although the Asante have elaborate temples, shrines, and altars, they do not worship God directly with these elements. Instead, they direct their worship in the temples and shrines to God through the intermediation of the ancestors and the lesser gods, and the spirits. Sarpong adds:

---

[135] S. A. Thorpe, *African Traditional Religion: An Introduction*, (Pretoria: University of South Africa, 1991), 1-2.
[136] Mbiti, *African Religions,* (New York: Praeger, 1969), 59. (See appendix F-H)

> If worship is defined in terms of temples and priests, then little worship is given to God. Rarely are temples built for Him. Images of God are almost non-existent, but there are countless representations of the other gods, in wood, clay, brass, and stone.[137]

Although the temples and altars in the Asante religion are not used directly to worship God but the intermediaries such as the ancestors and the lesser gods, the Asante have a separate altar for God. The altar that is used for God is different from those used to direct worship through the intermediaries.

The altars which are used for the offerings to God are in the shape of a forked branch cut from a certain tree. This tree altar is erected in front of the room of the owner of a house. Parrinder adds:

> It is hardly an exaggeration to say that every compound in Ashanti contains an altar to the sky God, in the shape of a forked branch cut from a certain tree which the Ashanti call "Nyame dua" literally "God's tree." This forked branch holds a brass or earthenware pot containing ancient stones (Neolithic celts) called "Nyame akuma" "God's axe." People put daily offerings in these pots, or on the roofs of their huts, for the Great God of the sky.[138]

It is generally believed among the Asante that worship is not offered to God directly because He is great and unapproachable, so people go to God through their intermediaries. I have a problem with this issue in that if the ancestors and the lesser gods are intermediaries, why do the Asante create two different altars? One to the intermediary and the other to the high God!

The Concept of Priesthood

Just as the Israelite religion had the office of priesthood, the Asante religion also believes in a priesthood as well. Although

---

[137] Sarpong, *Ghana in Retrospect*, 12.
[138] Geoffrey Parrinder, *West African Religion*, (London: The Epworth Press, 1961). 15.

the Israelite religion had male priests, the Asante religion believes in priests and priestesses (male and female).[139] Sarpong agrees with Mbiti that:

> The need for priests and priestesses, however, is an exigency which no change of environment can take away. The priesthood is a vital element in the worship of the gods. Every respectable deity has at least one priest or priestess. The sex of the ministers is not the index of the sex of the deity.[140]

The Asante priest's dress code is white (robe and white clay powder) with golden ornaments.

> Finely decorated temples of 'Nyame,' God, some of which were in the old Ashanti palaces. Priests wore gold or silver ornaments suspended from their necks, like enlarged crescents, with embossed motifs suggesting sun, moon, and stars. Priests had peculiar styles of hairdressing; white clay lines were drawn in the center of the forehead, and on shoulders, arms, and chest. They were dedicated for life service to the god.[141]

Moreover, the Asante priest assists the Asantehene in performing the purification rites and also pours libation as he makes intercessory prayer for the state and society and communicates with the ancestors. According to Adams:

> "The priest plays a key role in all the other rituals. The priest had a prophetic role, with the ability to make prophetic utterances under the inspiration of the gods. The priest's credibility depends on the truth or falsity of prophecies that he utters."[142]

The Concept of Sacrifice

So far, the study has introduced both personal and community practices of sacrifice in the Asante traditional religion to enable the reader to understand the Asante religion.

---

[139] Mbiti, *Introduction of African Religion*, 145.
[140] Sarpong, *Ghana in Retrospect*, 16.
[141] Geoffrey Parrinder, *West African Religion*, (London: The Epworth Press, 1961), 15.
[142] Adams, *Odwira and the Gospel*, 196.

The next section of the study will delineate a list of some sins regarded as religious sins in the Asante traditional religion. Also, the reader will be led into case studies of some religious sins under the main topic.

The Asante like the Israelites believe that sacrifice is one of the acts of worship by which humans acknowledge God to be near and approachable. Other acts include offerings, prayers, and invocation.[143] Mbiti states that, "African peoples respond to the spiritual world through sacrifices and offerings."[144] Parrinder also supports the idea that sacrifices of various drinks, fowl, or animals are made to turn away ancestors' anger. Drink sacrifices may consist of libations of water, rum, beer, and small quantities of food.[145]

The pouring of libations always accompanies an address to the spirits. For instance, and as Busia puts it, in the case of unintentional homicide where a hunter mistakenly shoots a man thinking it was a beast that was disturbing the bush, the hunter has to sacrifice a sheep for purification. When the sheep is sacrificed, the chief's spokesman addresses the spirits saying:

> *Obi na wato tuo bone, na yeahwehwe asem no mu. Ommoapa na yese onkosie nipa no. Yesremo, momma asemmone se eyi bi mma bio.* Someone has fired a bad gun; we have investigated the matter, he did not do it intentionally, and we say he should go and bury the man. We pray you not to let such a misfortune (bad thing) happen again.[146]

This is an example of a prayer that goes with the sacrifice of a sheep to avert any calamity that the anger of the deities might bring on a community in which a hunter had mistakenly killed a person in the bush.

Parrinder adds that, "An Asante farmer in West Africa, at the beginning of cultivation, brings offerings of a fowl and cooked yam for the spirit of the earth and his ancestors."[147] The act of

---

[143] Mbiti, *African Religions,* 33.
[144] Ibid. 61.
[145] Parrinder, *African Traditional Religion,* 38. (See appendix M).
[146] Busia, 71. For the chief spokesman's staff of authority.
[147] Parrinder, *African Traditional Religion,* 61, 83, 87.

sacrifice marks the point where the visible and invisible worlds meet, and show the human's intention to project himself into the invisible world.

When blood is shed in sacrifice, it means that "human or animal life is being given back to God who is in fact ultimate source of all life."[148] The worship of the Asante is neither formal nor regular, unlike systems of worship in a Christian gathering on Sunday morning 9:00 a.m. or the Muslims' prayers that must be offered five times a day. Sacrifice and offerings are acts of restoring the ontological balance between God and human, the spirits and human, departed and the living. When this balance is upset, people experience misfortunes and sufferings, or fear that these will come upon them. Sacrifices and offerings help, at least psychologically, to restore this balance.

When the sacrifices and offerings are directed toward the departed, they are a symbol of fellowship, recognition that the departed are still members of their human families, and tokens of respect and remembrance of the departed. The departed who are still remembered personally by someone in their family are the chief recipients of sacrifices and offerings from the family group. In this regard the Asante offer food and wine sacrifices.[149] Grillo shows how sacrifice connects both the living and the dead in good relationships. She says:

> In African religions, blood sacrifice shows life's dependence on death and establishes the reciprocal bond between spiritual and mortal realms. In African religions the life force released through blood sacrifice "feeds" the gods and the 'living dead' (ancestors) even as it channels their animating energy to the human community. A devotee must not forget the ritual duties that sustain this relationship; divinities and ancestors, while supportive are also demanding and can trouble a negligent supplicant by causing illness or chronic misfortune. In this way the ancestors, especially, are referred to as the guardians of the moral order. Reciprocity, at the heart of sacrificial exchange, sustains this order, making sacrifice an essentially

---

[148] Mbiti, *Introduction,* 5, 59.
[149] Mbiti, *Concept of God,* 178, 179, 192.

ethical act. Sacrifice, often a mute enactment, is an eloquent rhetorical device and powerful act, self-consciously wrought, to elicit the good for oneself in concert with community and divinity.[150]

The Asante believe that blood is the most precious gift in regard to the sacred. Therefore, blood seals all covenants, and once blood is shed for the deities, they are pleased to accept any request. In this case, the Asante is ready to release blood when the situation warrants such in their relationship with the deities. They believe that blood could be used to save a person from dying as the result of a deity's anger. This makes sacrifice, especially animal sacrifice, so important to the Asante.

The Concept of Prayer

The Asante make prayers sometimes without sacrifice but these prayers are accompanied with the pouring of a libation. People pour libation when they are happy as well as when they are unhappy. The time of libation is when people request the deities (God, the earth, the ancestors, and the tutelary spirits) to remember their subjects, and to bring the deities contact with what the people are doing. This means that the act of pouring a libation helps to acknowledge the existence of these deities:

> In pouring libation, therefore, the people are saying: *Here is an occasion which is significant and very important.* It may be an occasion of joy or sorrow and so on. Whatever it is, the people do not want to leave out their spiritual overlords . . . Libation therefore, *keeps the religious nature of human person always fresh in the Ghanaian's mind.*[151]

Most Asante prayers are said alongside a libation, and according to the passage cited above, pouring a libation in prayers is a sign of showing respect and to call the attention of a deity to a life situation whether joyful or sorrowful. Sarpong continues by saying:

---

[150] Grillo, "African Rituals," 122.
[151] Peter K. Sarpong, *Odd Customs, Stereotypes and Prejudices,* (Accra-Ghana: Sub-Saharan, 2012), 74.

Libation is the pouring forth of wine or other liquid in honor of a god or goddess, or for some other purpose. That libation is a practice that has been part of Ghana from time immemorial. No function of importance takes place without being preceded by libation. This function can be religious or social or cultural or even sporting. It can be collective, in the sense that it is being performed by a group of people or even the nation, or it can be private, in the sense that it may be only one person performing the function[152]

The Asante mention the name of God in their prayers though they seem also to ask the divinities to grant them health, prosperity, and protection from misfortune and witches. Although this example is not part of *asham* sacrifice I want the reader to see the way the Asante prayers are said, how they begin and the lines they follow. Note that the name of God is mentioned first followed by the other spirits. For example, the following is a mother's prayer at an Asante girl's puberty rite:

Onyankopon Tweaduampon Nyame, gye nsa nom. Asaase Yaa, gye nsa nom. Asamanfo, monye nsa nom. Obaa yi a Onyankopon de ama me yi, nne na wabo no bara. Oni a owo samando ommefa no onnye b ara nwu. Onyankopon Tweaduampon Nyame, receive this palm – wine and drink. Thursday Earth-Goddess, receive this palm-wine and drink. Ancestral spirits, receive this palm-wine and drink. This girl whom God has given me has menstruated today. Let not the Mother who dwells in the spirit-world take her away and causeher to have menstruated only to die.[153]

The next example provides a look at a husband's prayer at a curious rite during a young wife's first pregnancy:

Tweaduampon Nyame, Bosommuru, me bosom, me kra, moma akoda yi mmera dwo, 'O Tweaduampon Nyame, O Bosommuru, O my *obosom*, O my soul, let this child come forth quietly."[154]

---

[152] Ibid. 70.
[153] Evans, 251.
[154] Ibid.

These samples of two different kinds of prayer enable the reader to see that in the Asante traditional religion, prayers are said to the deities either to request something or to show appreciation.

The Concept of the Victim for *Asham* Sacrifice

Like the Israelites, the Asante *asham* sacrifice also has victims for sacrifice. Busia notes in the case studies of Asante on *asham* sacrifice in his book, *The Position of Chief in Ashanti* that the only sacrificial victim prominent in all the cases is a sheep.[155] According to Sarpong, a sheep, therefore, has a great sacrificial, purificatory, and worship value among Asante because it is considered an "innocent"- animal, which is -"peaceful,"- as opposed to, for example, the -"mischievous"- goat. A white sheep represents purity of heart and of the intention of the offerer. The use of sheep for sacrifices, therefore, symbolizes the sacrificer's desire for peace, and as peace and happiness are opposed to the disorder and hardship which *kyiribra (nubility rite)* occasions, the prominence of sheep at *kyiribra* purification ceremony appears to be both appropriate and necessary to the Ashanti. It signifies and initiates the return of the community to the state of guiltlessness.[156] The same attributes of a white sheep for sacrifice is still held in the Asante view today.

Other Types of Sacrifices

Other sacrifices are preventive, substitutionary, thanksgiving, votive, and foundation offerings.

A *preventive* offering is prescribed as a precautionary measure to prevent danger or disaster. For example, when a community learns that an epidemic is raging in a nearby village, it may offer this sacrifice to prevent the scourge from entering in its village.

A *substitutionary* offering has an element of propitiation and prevention. It is offered in place of the person who might have suffered some kind of misfortune. It may be offered to avert danger or misfortune that might befall someone. The sacrificial victim is rubbed against the body of the offerer to transfer the illness

---

[155] Busia, 71-73.
[156] Sarpong, *Girls' Nubility Rites,* 68.

or the misfortune to the victim. It is believed that the destiny of the offerer is exchanged, hence the term, *substitutionary* offering.

A *thanksgiving* offering is offered to express gratitude. The sacrifice accompanies a feast which brings the worshippers and the divinities together who share a communal meal.

A *votive* offering is a sacrifice of thanksgiving to express appreciation to a deity and also to fulfill a vow. This sacrifice is made when someone vows to give something to a deity if that deity helps him or her to achieve success in something. When the person is successful, he or she offers this sacrifice to thank the deity and at the same time fulfills his or her vow.

A *foundation* offering is offered at the beginning of projects such as the foundation of a house, the starting of a business, or a site of new land for cultivation. Such a sacrifice prevents evil spirits from entering the place.[157] The one offering the sacrifice can do so to the deity for protection so that every activity of the evil spirits will be curbed. Also, at the beginning of a business, the project can be given into the hands of the deity so that the beginning of the project and its progress will be secure. We will now examine the main topic of this chapter, the Asante *asham* sacrifice.

Asham Sacrifice

The Asante have two types of offences, according to Sarpong, private transgression and public offences. The private offences include theft (adultery and certain sexual acts are regarded as theft), certain kinds of assault, property cases, loans, and debts, etc. Sarpong stresses that "any of these offences can become a public offence when one of the parties concerned would swear an oath and the other replies in defiance or to maintain his innocence."[158] Sarpong continues by noting that a private offence committed by someone against a member of the same lineage is settled in the clan, and he explains further that public offences are regarded as those against the community as a whole. As such

---

[157] Deji, Ayegboyin. "Sacrifice" *Encyclopedia of African Religion.* 2:583-584.
[158] Sarpong, *Ancestral Stool*, 161.

they are directly against the ancestors and so are religious transgressions punishable in the past by death, banishment, or very heavy fines.[159]

Sarpong agrees with Busia's list of culpable offences in the Asante religion and reproduces the same list.[160] According to Deji Ayegboyin, *asham* is also a sacrifice offered when a worshipper violates a prohibition. He gives an example from among the Akans (the larger group of which Asante is part):

> if a man indulges in sexual intercourse in the bush, it is believed that, the two people have defiled themselves and that their defilement has affected the Earth goddess: therefore, she has to be propitiated. On such occasions, sacrifice should be offered at the sacred grove to propitiate the Earth mother and ancestors.[161]

There are many offences in Asante that call for *asham* sacrifice. K. A. Busia[162] and Peter Sarpong[163] describe the classes of offences which require *asham* sacrifice. When a person fails to control the tongue or speech for instance when in the presence of a member of a royal house, the person must first say *Sebe oo!* "Excuse me please!" If one infringes this rule, one has caused defilement to the crown and the land. In response a sheep must be slaughtered as a sacrifice. When a person swears an illicit oath, for example, the oath of a king or a chief which no one is allowed to swear except a rightful royal, such a person will be compelled to kill a sheep for sacrifice before the person is tried for the infringement of royal person. Similarly if someone accidentally kills a person, or a person commits suicide, or causes a serious injury to self, a sheep must be sacrificed to the ancestors to purge the misfortune. If there is incest, or an adulterous relationship with a chief's wife, the male offender must bring a sheep for sacrifice to appease the ancestors and the gods.

---

[159] Ibid. 162.
[160] Ibid.
[161] Adegboyin, "Sacrifice" 2:583.
[162] Busia, 70-72.
[163] Sarpong, *Girl's Nubility Rites,* 60-72.

Likewise, if one transgresses against a chief, for instance by cursing him, the oblation of a sheep to the ancestors is very necessary. Busia shows that the offences over which the chief takes cognizance are religious offences. The list of those offences was drawn up by the Asante Confederacy Council at 1946.[164] These are offences for which the native courts demand the slaughter of sheep because they are religious and therefore cause defilement to the land. The list follows in Table 1 below.

Table 1. Offences Drawn Up By The Asante Confederacy Council at 1946.

A. *Offences against stool and traditional office-holders.*
1. Insulting and assaulting of state dignitaries (i.e. traditional office-holders).
2. Assault or fighting in the house of a State dignitary.
3. Cursing any individual, or a State dignitary.
4. Exchange of blows between two State dignitaries.
5. Having sexual intercourse with the wife of a State dignitary.
6. A State dignitary putting himself or being put into fetish.
7. A woman in her menstrual period entering the house of a State dignitary.
8. Disrespecting an oath which had been sworn.
9. Treason (*epo*).
10. Cowardice (*dwanedom:* flee from the enemy's troop).
11. Commands enjoined with the chief's oath.
12. Assault on the chief, his soul-washer, stool-carrier, or keeper of his mausoleum.
13. Stealing from the chief (*krono kese*).
14. Abusing the chief.

B. *Sexual offences.*
1. Incest.
2. Having sexual connection with a woman in the bush.
3. Having sexual connection with a woman during her menstrual period.

---

[164] Busia, 149.

4. Having sexual connection with a pregnant woman who is not one's wife.
5. A woman swearing an oath during her menstrual period.
6. Swearing the oath to deny a sexual act which had in fact taken place.

C. *Offences against the gods.*
1. Entering or polluting a sacred grove or shrine or stream.
2. Stealing from the gods.
3. Witchcraft (*bayie*).
4. Other taboos.

D. *Murder*
1. Suicide by hanging (*hye akomfo*); by wounding oneself (*di wo ho awu*).
2. Unintentional homicide (*obi annhye da kum obi a*).[165]

Just as the Israelites have classified wrongdoing into sin and reparation, the Asante also classify wrong-doing into religious and non-religious offences. The Maasai people of Kenya also have classified wrongdoing into *Bad Deeds, intorrok* and *Sins, ing'ok.*[166]

Table 2. Offences among the Maasai

1. Thievery.
2. Insulting or continually abusing people.
3. Adultery, which is seen as a form of thievery.
4. Cursing people.
5. Hitting a crippled person or a blind person.
6. Not giving food to those who are hungry.
7. Insulting people due to drunkenness.
8. Having a mean disposition.
9. Not caring for the herds.
10. Shooting an animal so that it dies very slowly.

---

[165] Busia, 70, 150.
[166] Priest, 54, 158-168.

11. Killing bees while taking honey.
12. Observing snakes copulating.
13. Failure to treat the elderly with respect.
14. Beating one's relative with a knobkerrie.

A Listing of Sins Includes

1. Murdering another person.
2. A son not having peace with his family.
3. Not paying the fine for killing another Maasai.
4. The killing of an animal such as a dog by one who is circumcised.
5. Cursing a Maasai for no appropriate reason.
6. Sending a wife away when she has done nothing.
7. A parent having intercourse with his or her offspring.

Some Case Studies of Offence in Asante Religion

Now that we have seen the list of the various offences that demand *asham* sacrifice and given some indication of the methods and times of such sacrifice, let us examine some cases from offences listed above from K. A. Busia's record.

On September 26, 1941, a meeting was held in Kumasi during which the Asantehene appeared in state. The chiefs, who had come from their divisions to attend a meeting of the Confederacy,[167] were present. One of them, the Dormaahene, had a chair (*asipim*) with gold bands on it. No one in Asante apart from the Asantehene is allowed to have his stool adorned with gold. In olden days this breach of etiquette would have led to a war. (It was the ostensible cause of war against Adinkra, King of Jaman, in 1818).[168] The Dormaahene, however, apologized through the Kokofuhene. Although he was forgiven, he was asked to slaughter twelve sheep. The offence was considered an offence against the ancestors, and the sheep had to be sacrificed to appease them. No one should make himself equal to the Asantehene, who alone is the successor of his royal ancestors.[169]

---

[167] The Asante Confederacy or the Asanteman Council is composed of Paramount Chiefs in the Asante Region and the four senior divisional chiefs of Kumase state. (Osei, *An Outline,* 9-10).
[168] Busia, *The Position of Chief in Ashanti,* 96-97.
[169] Ibid.

The commission of sexual offences under the religious list is regarded as something which defiles the earth and offends the gods and the ancestors. Unless offenders are tried and punished, the earth purified, and the ancestors appeased by sacrifice, the community will suffer. For example, hunters would fail to kill animals in the forest, the crops would refuse to bear fruit, the spirits of the dead ancestors would be infuriated, the gods would be angered, clans would cease to exist, and all would be chaos in the world.[170]

In a case which came before a chief in 1934, at a place 24 miles from Kumasi, a girl was found pregnant although her puberty rites had not been performed. The man concerned was sent for and asked to bring a sheep. The sheep was killed, and some of its blood was sprinkled on the two offenders. They were then driven out of the town amidst shouts of derision. They lived in a hut away from the town and were not allowed to return until forty days after the baby was born.[171]

Another case happened in 1935 in another town close to Kumasi. A young man had sexual intercourse with a girl whose puberty rites had not been performed. In this instance she was not pregnant. The young man provided a sheep which was sacrificed to the Earth and the ancestors, with the prayer that they might accept the sheep and avert any misfortune which the crime might have occasioned. The man was then beaten severely, the elders having decided that this was a more effective way than imposing a fine on him after the sacrifice was made.

Sexual intercourse with one of the same blood or clan, with a woman in the bush even if it is with one's own wife, with a woman who is pregnant, with a girl who had not reached puberty, or with a woman during her menstrual period, are all offenses for which the male offender must bring a sheep to be sacrificed in the open space where the court sits. This offering is to appease the ancestors and the gods and to cleanse the earth, which was believed to have been defiled.[172]

---

[170] Ibid. 71.
[171] Ibid. 72.
[172] Ibid.

In the case of murder, a hunter unintentionally shot a man he saw disturbing the bush and mistook him for a beast. If the elders found that this was in fact an accident, the man who was responsible for the misadventure was asked to give a sheep which was sacrificed on the ancestral stools of the chief, the Okyeame. The chief's spokesperson would address the spirits thus:

Obi nawatotuo bone, na yeahwehwe asem no mu. Ommoapa na yese onkosie nipa no. Yesre mo, momma asem bone se eyi mma bio. Meaning, someone has fired a bad gun; we have investigated the matter, he did not do it intentionally, and we say he should go and bury the deceased. We pray you not let such a misfortune (bad thing) happen again.[173]

A glance through these cases has shown that the Asante understand that the ancestors and gods are sacred and therefore holy. The next section will treat further Asante's ideas and values in sacrifice.

Objects of Sacrifice for *Asham* Offering in the Asante Traditional Religion

The Asante *asham* sacrifice has victims for sacrificial offering. It could be observed from the case studies on *asham* sacrifice of Asante given in the section above that, the only sacrificial victim prominent in all the cases is a sheep.[174] As already noted, the use of sheep for sacrifices therefore symbolizes the sacrificer's desire for peace; and as peace and happiness are opposed to disorder and hardship which *kyiribra (nobility rite)* occasions, the prominence of sheep at *kyiribra* purification ceremony appears to be both appropriate and necessary to the Ashanti. It signifies and causes the return of the community to the state of blamelessness.[175]

---

[173] Busia, 71-72.
[174] Busia, 71-73.
[175] Sarpong, *Girls' Nubility Rites,* 68.

Table 3. Objects with blood

(1) The herd: The Asante do not offer any animal from the herd. It is forbidden to offer cattle as sacrifice. But Asantehene would strike a cow three times with the state's sword which is the totem of the Asantehene on behalf of the state to give way to the ritual of purification at Odwira festival.[176]

(2) The flock: sheep (white sheep).
Asante *asham* offering always demands a healthy sheep and ordinarily a white one.

(3) The fowl: Fowl can be used in other purifications but not in *asham* sacrifice.

Objects without blood

(1) The foodstuffs: Because the *asham* offering is not a celebration, no food is offered for *asham* offering.

(2) The liquid: Wine and beer are used for libation.

(3) Other: There are no other types of objects prescribed for the *asham* offering in Asante. The Asante have different types of sacrifices, but in order to restore purity, peace, tranquility, and respect for God, and respect for fellow human being, the study has indicated that the *asham* sacrifice with its victim (sheep) have played a major role in the Asante society.

To summarize the discussion so far, one should note that the Asante *asham* sacrifice is not performed without ruling principles that guide the process. The study has revealed earlier that the Asante Confederacy selected all religious offenses that require an *asham* offering. Therefore, Asante *asham* sacrifice has rules and regulations which the offender, the priest, and other participants must follow. Sometimes where they lack knowledge, it is revealed to them through the oracles that the spirit of the gods or the ancestors may provide. In situations like this, everyone is very careful because the deities would not tolerate careless fumbling with their statutes. Although the Asante religion does not

---

[176] Adams, 45.

have its rules, commands, and statutes in written codes, structured laws and commands in the tradition are transmitted in oral codes. The king, the priests, and the elders learned these by hearing repeated reference made to them. However, today many priests, kings and elders are educated, so some, if not all, are now written down.

Consequently, the priest would have to invite the deities to come and take control and to register their acceptance of the sacrifice; priests have different styles for this process, according to the revelation that he or she has received. On some occasions the participants in sacrifice sing and beat drums. It is very important to share Louise Francoise Müller's[177] experience in Kumasi at one of the *Akomfo* (priests) dances. She says that the priestesses dance inside a circle to the tune of talking drums to invoke natural deities. The drums send messages from the living to the spiritual beings because it is believed that the spiritual beings are familiar with the language of the drums. Müller stresses that the Asante traditional priests invite good spirits from outside their local spiritual realm to cure their patients because they believed that evil spirits are also located outside their spiritual realm. Also, the priests and priestesses use bodily movements as the main medium of communication. As they dance along, they fall into a trance in which is believed that the deities come upon them and send messages to the people. They dance to show their ultimate power in dealing with the spiritual beings. Müller was fascinated by the scene and says:

> The traditional priests or priestesses show that they are in control of the beings of the spiritual realm by calling upon the four cardinal points as part of their *akom* dancing. They first point to the sky, which is North representing the High God *(Nyame);* then, they point to the South, which is the Earth Goddess *(AsaseYaa);* to the West, to acknowledge the powers of the ancestors *(Nananom nsamanfoD)* and to the East, to recognize the forces of the other deities. Finally, they point to the centre, which represents the traditional priests and priestesses.

---

[177] Louise Francoise Müller, "Dancing Golden Stools: Indigenous Religion as a Strategy for Identity Construction in Ghana," *FIR* 5.1 (2010): 32-57.

The meaning of the directions in dancing is to show that "except for the High God" *(Gye Nyame)* in the Sky, who is often compared with the wind and the Earth Goddess *(Asase Yaa)*, the traditional priests and priestesses have power over the beings of the spiritual world. In the demonstration of their spiritual powers, Ashanti priests and priestesses have also built in a competitive element in their demonstration of the spirits with which they communicate through spiritual possession. Ashanti priests are therefore well-known for their dangerous acts, such as the eating of hot charcoal, the pounding of *fufu* (mashed yam) on a priest's back or the swallowing of a raw egg.[178]

This experience of Müller and others bears out the fact that the Asante *asham* sacrifices play a great part in the Asante society.

Conclusion

Asante traditional religion involves ancestral worship. The Asante believe that the inhabitants on the universe include human beings, spirits, and a Supreme Being. The Asante believe that God created everything, but the spirits and the gods are intermediaries between God and humans. They believe that their worship goes to the great God through the intermediaries. There are temples, shrines, and altars made of stone, mud, and more elaborate images. There priests acquire knowledge by consulting the gods to come and speak to them. Other objects such as beads, amulets, are used as charms and fetishes. The Asante believe that plants and animals may be appealed to because they are inhabited by spirits. They believe in the existence of hostile spirits from which black magic and witchcraft come.

Sacrifice, especially the expiatory sacrifice, is made for many purposes such as sin, reparation, purification for nubility, and cleansing the dead. Sheep and fowl are the main blood sacrificial victims; yams and eggs are objects for food sacrifice, while wine, beer, and sometimes water are objects for liquid sacrifice to pour libations.

---

[178] Müller, 42.

Some of the causes for Asante sacrifices are crises like epidemics, famine, drought, or serious illness and violation of a prohibition. Most sacrifices are made to calm the anger of the gods. The Asante recognize the sacred and the profane, hence the *asham* sacrifice for purging the offerer from wrong-doing. The Asante classify wrong-doing into religious and non-religious offences. They classify all religious infractions as sins that defile the community, the individual, and any defilement that mars the relationship between god and humans. An appropriate *asham* sacrifice is always prescribed to purge the offender from sin and restore peace in the community. All these are for restoring and maintaining good relationships between deities and their human worshippers.

The Asante believe that God is near and approachable. Along with sacrifice, other rituals include offerings, prayers, and invocations. Sacrifices and offerings to the departed are symbols of fellowship and recognition that the departed are still members of a human family. Food and drinks given to the departed are tokens of fellowship, hospitality, and respect. The Asante have totems and taboos.

The Asante have other types of sacrifices such as preventive, substitutionary, votive, and foundation offerings, which however are the subject of further studies. Expiatory sacrifices include Odwira, which is a period of cleansing the spirit of the nation and the ancestral properties. Odwira is discussed in this chapter. The *asham* sacrifice is offered when there is violation of a prohibition. The lists of sins that require *asham* offering have been illustrated, and some case studies of offences requiring *asham* offering have been provided.

It can be concluded that the Ashanti religious ideas regarding sacrifice are very similar to those of the Israelites, but the specific practices that embody those ideas are different. As in Israelite practice, the Asante have an *asham* sacrifice in order to purge individuals and sacred belongings from the contaminations that come from sin.

Chapter 4: Similarities and Dissimilarities

In this chapter, I will discuss the similarities and dissimilarities of *asham* sacrifice between the Israelite and Asante religions. I will leave any judgment or decision in the hands of the reader and provide some recommendations. Meanwhile, we shall look at the similarities of *asham* sacrifice notably in regard to areas such as the holy things of God and human-to-human relationships.

The study will reveal the areas where the two religions have different ways of putting these similar ideas into practice. This will call for the reader to use his or her judgment in order to ascertain constructive theological implications from the study.

Similarities

Evidently, the two religions hold similar ideas in some areas. *First*, their commonality dwells on the idea of the One who created everything, and they share the idea that this Creator deserves worship. Israelite Holy Scriptures begin with the expression *Bereshith bara Elohim et hashamayim va-et ha-arets*, "In the beginning God created heaven and earth" (Gen 1:1). The Asante similarly believe that the High God in the sky is the Creator, the Giver of life, sun, and rain. Sarpong says, "It is evidently because God is the Creator and continuous Originator of life that in public sacrifices; even when they are offered to idols and ancestors, He is usually invoked before everyone."[179] Molefi Kete Asante agrees with Sarpong that "Nyankopon is the creator of all gods and so many golden objects are symbolic of his radiance."[180]

Second, they both have the idea of covenantal relationship with their deities. Yahweh made a covenant with the Israelites through their forefather Abraham in Gen 17:1-3, and the covenant was sealed with human male circumcision (Gen 17:9-14). This covenant was extended to Isaac (Gen 26:1-5), and then to Jacob and his children (Gen 35:9-12). The Asante priests and devotees also enter into covenant relationship with their deities. Adams and Sarpong agree that the priests are possessed by the

---

[179] Sarpong, *Ghana in Retrospect*, 11.
[180] Asante and Nwadiora, 10.

deities: "This utilitarian outlook of Ghanaians on their gods affords an explanation as to why the latter apparently alter their functions and qualities with a change of environment and ownership."[181] This is not just a deep relationship but a covenant with a seal according to the symbol of each deity.

Third, according to many biblical texts Yahweh told the Israelites not to use anything on earth or heaven to represent Him as an image or symbol of Him (notably Exod 20:4; Deut 5:8). The Asante also believe that the Creator has no image; therefore, they made no representation of *Onyankopon:* "Images of God are non-existent … The true Ghanaian would laugh if one spoke of the possibility of representing God in art."[182]

Fourth, Israelites believe that sacrilege against Yahweh and His holy things and some offences against a fellow human being are regarded as religious infractions that require an *asham* sacrifice (Lev 5:14-6:7; 14:10-12; 19:20-22). The Asante also believe that some offences are religiously committed whereby the civil courts could not sit at the case but rather the religious personnel such as the chief and priests.

As Sarpong puts it:
> The latter category of sin is classified as taboos, and in the olden days the penalty for their disregard was death, a very heavy fine or perpetual banishment. As they were said to have estranged or threatened the ancestors or the gods of the community and so imperil its well-being; those who offended against these taboos were, in time past, tried by the king or chief, and their trial began with the sacrifice of sheep to the ancestors, the gods and the Supreme Being who were thought to have been infuriated.[183]

On the same issue of how the Asante view sacredness, Sarpong says, "Libation reminds us of the sacredness of the environment."[184] The Asante belief in the sacredness of the Kingship and the gods and the things pertaining to them is so strong that

---

[181] Sarpong, *Ghana in Retrospect,* 17. Adams, 196.
[182] Ibid. 12.
[183] Ibid. 54.
[184] Sarpong, *Odd Customs,* 75.

women in their menstrual period were not allowed to go near these sacred entities. Kwadwo Osei confirms that:

> If those rules were not observed, they led to serious consequences for the state. For example, in the olden days, when a woman was in her menstrual period, she was forbidden from visiting our stool houses. There were rivers a woman in her menses could not cross or go to fetch water. They were forbidden from cooking for their husbands. When women were in their menses they had to show by painting the left wrist with white clay.[185]

Fifth, the worship of Yahweh required the service of priests in the Temple in Israel. To accomplish this demand, Yahweh instructed that priests must be ordained. In Exodus 28:1-43 priests were chosen to serve in the house of Yahweh. The Asante religious worship required the service of priests in many contexts and particularly in the *asham* offering. As Adams puts it:

> "The traditional priest *akomfo* plays a key role in the Asante Odwira festival ... The priest is charged with religious duties in the temple, shrine and sacred grove ... the traditional priest played a key role in all other rituals ... The *okomfo* is therefore, a leader in every aspect of life."[186]

Sixth, the Israelites worshipped Yahweh in the temple (Exod 25-30; 1 Kgs 5-8). The Asante likewise have the idea of worshipping their deity in a temple. Adams previously noted that, "The priest is charged with religious duties in the temple, shrine and sacred grove".[187] This supports the idea that the Asante hold the idea of worshipping in a temple. Parrinder describes the temples as:

> Finely decorated temples of "Nyame," some of which were in the old Asante palaces. Priests wore gold or silver ornaments suspended from their necks, like enlarged crescents, with embossed motifs suggesting sun, moon and stars. Priests had peculiar styles of hairdressing; white clay lines were drawn in the center of the forehead,

---

[185] Osei, *Asante Culture,* 12.
[186] Adams, 196.
[187] Ibid.

and on shoulders, arms, and chest. They were dedicated for life of service to god ... The Ashanti are unique in West Africa not in honoring a Supreme Being, but in having temples, priests, and altars to Him ... There are only a few temples of God, found almost exclusively in Ashanti.[188]

Seventh, Chapter 2 showed that the Israelites have five different kinds of sacrifices in Leviticus 5-7, of which the *asham* sacrifice is one that plays a major function in the relationship between Yahweh and the Israelites. In Israel, the *asham* sacrifice is the sacrifice required when someone commits a sacrilege against Yahweh. In the same vein, the Asante also have the sacrifice which they offer to appease the Supreme Being and the other spirits to keep the relationship between the sacred and profane moving smoothly. According to Sarpong:

> The latter category of sins is classified as taboos, and in the olden days the penalty for their disregard was death, a very heavy fine or perpetual banishment. As they were said to have estranged or threatened to estrange the ancestor or the gods from the community and so imperil its well-being, those who offended against these taboos were, in time past, tried by the king or chief, and their trial began with the sacrifice of sheep to the ancestors, the gods and the Supreme Being who were thought to have been infuriated.[189]

Eighth, in Israel, the object of the *asham* sacrifice was a ram without defect. The animal prescribed by Yahweh for the *asham* offering was exclusively a ram from the flock, one without defect and of proper value in silver. The value was standardized by way of the sanctuary shekel (5:15, 18; 6:6; 19:22). Also, there needed to be restitution, plus an additional twenty percent of the value of what the person had failed to do in regard to the holy things (5:16), or the item of a neighbor that was affected (6:4-6). Similarly, the Asante have a victim for their *asham* sacrifice, a sheep. This sacrifice goes with the pouring of libation too, as Sarpong explains further:

---

[188] Parrinder, *West African Religion*, 15, 25.
[189] Sarpong, *Ghana in Retrospect*, 53-54.

Sins against the ancestors are sometimes put right by the pouring of wine on the ancestral stools and the sacrifice of sheep. When somebody commits incest for which the penalty used to be death or banishment it is now commuted to a fine and payment of several sheep, the blood of the sacrificed animal is poured on the ancestral stools.[190]

The Asante sacrifice requires a healthy sheep which is expressed in the Asante language "Odwan pa a otua dua!" which literally means "a good sheep with tail" or, "a healthy sheep with no deformity."[191]

Dissimilarities

Thus far, we have noted the similar ideas that the Israelite and the Asante religions have about *asham* sacrifice. The reality must not be overlooked, however, that there are significant differences in the practice of each of the religions. The *first point* of differences between the two religions concerns the reality of the concept of covenantal relationship.

As we have seen in the study above, the Israelites were called and chosen by Yahweh to be His nation and people:

> And Moses went up to God, and the LORD called to him from the mountain saying, "Thus you shall say to the house of Jacob, and tell the children of Israel: You have seen what I did to the Egyptians, and how I bore you on eagles' wings and brought you to myself. Now therefore, if you will indeed obey my voice and keep my covenant, then you shall be a special treasure to Me above all people; for all the earth is mine. And you shall be to me a kingdom of priests and a holy nation. These are the words which you shall speak to the children of Israel." (Exod 19:3-6)

But there is no indication that Yahweh had any covenant relationship with the Asante. Even their religious principles show that the Asante regard God as too great to approach; therefore,

---

[190] Sarpong, Ancestral Stools, 25.
[191] *Emphasis mine.* (It is generally expressed in that way among the Asante).

they approach Him through intermediaries such as lesser gods and ancestors. As Kwadwo Osei puts it:

> In addition to the believe [sic] in God, the Asantes believe in lesser gods like rivers, mountains, lakes, mighty trees, such as Oak tree, and climbing stems like: Ahomatere or Ahomakyem. They believe that the items mentioned have superior spirits in them and are therefore treated as spokesmen to the supreme God so they pass their prayers through them to God. The Asantes who adhere to the teachings of our traditional religion offer sacrifices to the supreme God on the altars of the lesser gods. The belief is that the lesser gods would carry the sacrifices to the supreme God.[192]

The Asante traditionalists were not called by Yahweh but rather called by the deities. As Sarpong puts it,

> Many priests attribute the adoption of their profession to possession by some spirit influence. They suddenly hear such and such a god calling them. They fall into a fit or a trance. Upon consultation, a qualified priest would interpret the phenomenon as meaning that the spirit of the god wants to marry you.[193]

Second, the Israelites believe that Yahweh alone must be worshipped: "Hear, O Israel: The LORD is one! You shall love the LORD your God with all your heart, with all your soul, and with all your strength." (Deut 6:4-6). Here, Moshe Weinfeld reveals that "the connotation of *one* here is not solely unity but also aloneness ... The word *one* (*ehad*) implies exclusiveness, as may be learned from 1 Chr 29:1, God has chosen my son Solomon alone."[194] Weinfeld stresses that such kind of liturgical confessional proclamation has been made by other deities in other societies apart from Israel. He says:

> Oneness in reference to a god involves aloneness may be learned from a proclamation about the god Enlil in a Sumerian dedication inscription: Enlil is the Lord of heaven and earth, he is king alone. Similarly, we read

---

[192] Osei, *A Handbook on Asante Culture*, 90.
[193] Sarpong, *Ghana in Retrospect*, 17.
[194] Weinfeld, 1991), 337.

about the god Baal or Mot in Ugaritic literature, "I am one [= alone] who rules over the gods, who rules over gods and men...By the same token, Deut 6:4 is a kind of liturgical confessional proclamation and by itself cannot be seen as monotheistic; it is its association with the first two commandments of the Decalogue and its connection with other proclamations in the sermons of Deuteronomy, such as Deut 10:17, that make it monotheistic. [195]

Patrick Miller agrees with Weinfeld that the God of Israel is understood to be one but notes that "The latter primarily of a contextual and historical character in that Deuteronomy is concerned with the sole worship of the Lord, not multiple manifestations of Israel's God."[196] Yahweh told the Israelites to have no other gods because He knew some had worshiped other gods, hence the command:

> You shall have no other gods before me. You shall not make for yourself a carved image-any likeness of anything that is in heaven above, or that is in the earth beneath, or that is in the water under the earth." (Deut 5:6-8; Exod 20:3-4). Yahweh says, "You shall not bow down to them nor serve them (Exod 20: 5a).

Contrary to the view articulated in the Pentateuch by various strands of Israelite theological reflection, Asante traditionalists, as Kwadwo Osei notes, believe in lesser gods who take their sacrifices to the supreme God. Osei describes at least one way in which such sacrifice works:

> There are also man-made deities built with a collection of some special leaves, barks of special trees, gold-dust and gold nuggets, all heaped in a basin and covered with clay. They sacrifice fowls and animals on the deities to appease the gods. [197]

Here, Osei is showing how a deity can be brought into existence by gathering certain materials together to become an abode of a spirit.

---

[195] Ibid. 338.
[196] Patrick Miller, *Deuteronomy: Interpretation, A Bible Commentary for Teaching and Preaching*, (Louisville: John Knox Press, 1990), 99.
[197] Ibid. 90.

Osei proposes that apart from the natural phenomena such as trees, mountains, rocks, and rivers etc. even in one's room, a deity can be introduced to be served as one gathers those materials together. As Sarpong puts it:

> The last group of minor deities is sometimes separated from the first three groups, for the lesser gods are graded in a regular descending scale until they reach or at times almost merge into those classes which are among the lowest grades of superhuman powers. Deities of that group differ from the rest in that they are articles of some sort which are worn or hung in the house for protective purposes. It is the belief in these which can be rightly termed "fetishism," a word derived from the Portuguese word, *fetico*, a charm.[198]

Third, the priesthood in Israel was assigned to one tribe, the tribe of Levi, and from the lineage of Aaron and his sons (Exod 28; 40:12-15; Lev 8; Num 4). That refers to male priests from the tribe of Levi alone officiated in the Israelite temple. On the contrary, the Asante priests could be chosen from anywhere in the society regardless of tribe and gender because "The need for priests and priestesses, however, is an exigency which no change of environment can take away."[199] The fact that the Asante religion has both male and female priests is clear. Also the priest of the Asante uses incantation alongside sacrifice with the pouring of libations. The procedure of the pouring of libation is shown by Osei:

> Here the person pouring libation calls the names of the powers i.e. He mentions the name of God Almighty and shows the container of the wine to the skies; he mentions the earth and pours a drop on the ground. He mentions the names of the deities one after the other or collectively and pours a drop on the ground. He mentions the names of the ancestors one after the other or collectively and pours a drop on the ground. Here he narrates the purpose of the libation e.g. The marriage and performance of rites or prayers to the powers that be, to avoid calamity

---

[198] Sarpong, *Ghana in Retrospect*, 14.
[199] Ibid. 17.

etc. Here he prays to the powers for help or for prosperity or protection. After the narration he curses his enemies.[200]

In contrast, the priest of Israel performed *asham* sacrifices without talking. Although this point is debated by some scholars, Knohl makes it clear that the priestly cult was a domain of silence. He uses several quotations to prove this point:

> In Egypt, Babylonia and in the pagan world in general, word and incantation were integral parts of the cult; act was accompanied by speech. The spell expressed the magical essence of cultic activity. In more developed form, pagan rituals might be accompanied by mythological allusions relating to events in the life of the gods. Speech thus articulated the magical-mythological sense of the rite. P makes no reference to the spoken word in describing temple rites. All the various acts of the priest are performed in silence. Not only have spells and psalms no place in the priestly cult, even prayer is absent. Priestly speech is found only outside the temple or apart from the essential cultic act. This silence is an intuitive expression of the priestly desire to fashion a non-pagan cult. Though the detail of the priestly rites, magical in origin and essence, could not be done away with, the magical motivation made explicit in the accompanying utterances was eliminated. Therewith the Israelite cult became a domain of silence.[201]

Knohl accepts the fact that around the circle of the priest in the Temple court other activities such as songs, prayers etc. took place:

> The priestly cult in the temple of silence could not contain the abundance of popular religious sentiment. Around the silent sanctuary throbbed the joyous popular cult, all tumult and passion. Prayer belonged almost exclusively to the popular religion; it is not mentioned in P. Ordinarily, the individual prays for himself. When, on occasion, an intercessor appears, he is not a priest, but a

---

[200] Osei, *A Handbook on Asante Culture*, 93-94.
[201] Knohl, "Between Voice and Silence: The Relationship between Prayer and Temple Cult." *JBL* 115/1 (1996): 17-30.

righteous man or prophet. The only prayer formulated in the Torah is the tithe-confession which is non-priestly.[202]

Knohl stresses that "Menahem Haran and Moshe Greenberg, even though they disagree in their evaluation of the position of prayer in relation to sacrifice, both accept the description of the priestly cult as a silent one."[203] Knohl makes his point clearer by explaining:

> Let me preface my discussion by stating that in my opinion the fundamental distinctions drawn by Kaufmann have a solid basis. However, the claim he has articulated pertains only to the inner circle of the priesthood. Beyond this circle, as Kaufmann himself has observed, there is no silence at all. Instead, we find the songs of the Levites and the shouting of the people.[204]

In a nutshell, Knohl makes an effort to inculcate the fact about silence in the temple and silence at the offering of sacrifice, arguing that "This combination of contrasting and complementary circles of silence and sound could only exist in the Temple, in whose center was conducted the silent service of the sacrifices, surrounded by the realm of hymn and prayer."[205]

In Asante, incantations and other demonstrations accompany the sacrifice, or rather, a sacrifice includes both the killing of an animal and several other activities. This is not the case in Israel's Temple cult.

A *fourth* difference is that in Asante, the king or chief is regarded as the chief priest who can perform rituals; this is not found in Israel. So, for example, when King Uzziah tried to burn incense in the temple of Yahweh, he was rebuked by Azariah the priest and eighty priests of Yahweh (2 Chron 26:17-18). By the Second Temple period, if not earlier, the human king was excluded from the Israelite temple cult.

Fifth, the worship of the Israelites according to the biblical traditions was performed in one Tabernacle or one Temple. Wor-

---

[202] Ibid.
[203] Ibid. 18.
[204] Ibid.
[205] Knohl, 24.

ship or sacrifices were officiated or led by the priests from Aaron's lineage. The Tabernacle was a mobile worship place during those wilderness journeys of Israel. The Temple was the permanent worship place of Yahweh when the Israelites settled in the Promised Land. The Temple was to be built in Jerusalem and the priests the sons of Aaron, were to officiate in it in Jerusalem. In the words of the Book of Tobit:

> Now when I was in my own country, in the land of Israel, while I was still a young man, the whole tribe of Naphtali my forefather deserted the house of Jerusalem. This is the place which has been chosen from among all the tribes of Israel, where all the tribes should sacrifice and where the Temple of the dwelling of the Most High was consecrated and established for all generations forever. Offerings are made by the priests the sons of Aaron at the altar. The Levites ministered at Jerusalem.[206]

The Israelites of Bible times worshipped Yahweh at one place in one Temple and on one altar. In the words of Sirach/Ecclesiasticus, we see that the Temple was renovated, "He laid the foundation for the high double wall, the high retaining wall of the temple precinct" (v. 2), the high priest performing his duties with the priests of Aaron's line in the Temple at the holy altar (v. 11-17).[207] The expression "the temple" in these passages indicates the singleness of a particular or definite temple. Unlike the Israelites who had only one Temple and one altar for the whole nation, the Asante have many temples and shrines where they worship their deities. According to Geoffrey Parrinder:

> Finely decorated temples and of 'Nyame,' God, some of which were in the old Ashanti palaces … The Ashanti are unique in West Africa in honoring a Supreme Being, but in having (many) temples, priests, and altars to him …"[208]

The temples of Asante are many because they worship many gods, and each god or goddess has a temple and an altar.

---

[206] Tobit 1:6, 7.
[207] Sirach/Ecclesiasticus 50:1-29.
[208] Parrinder, *West African Religion,* 15, 25.

Sixth, the types of sacrifices in Leviticus include the thanksgiving (Lev 1 and 2), the fellowship (Lev 2 and 3), the purification (Lev 4), the graduated (Lev 5:1-13), and the expiatory (Lev 5:1-6:7; 14:10-12; 19:20-22) sacrifices. The Asante have different types of sacrifices as well, but they do not have the graduated sacrifice where the status of a person or group of persons determines the kind of sacrifice to be offered (Lev 5:1-13).

Seventh, and the last point for the present, the Israelites use a ram without blemish and a fine of twenty percent of the item desecrated. The Asante have the same object, a healthy ram and a fine. The difference is that the Asante *asham* offering includes a ram, a fine that is not specified like that of the Israelites, and the pouring of libation accompanied by incantations. The Asante use palm wine or distilled wine or water to pray or pour the libation. In explaining how people are fined when they commit religious sin and they offer the *asham* sacrifice, for example, as in the case of a boy who impregnates a girl who has not performed puberty rites, Osei says:

> To avert any calamity that might result from that deed, the parents of both the boy and the girl would be summoned to the chief's palace where the chief would impose heavy fines on them as deterrent to others. The offenders would be brought before the people. The hair on their heads would be shaved and an egg would be broken on the head of each of them. A fowl would be killed and the blood sprinkled on them. A ram would also be slaughtered to appease the deities and the blood poured on their heads. The chief's linguist would then pronounce the following statement on them: "Mo mmusuo ngu mo ara mo tiri so." Being literally translated "The calamity you have caused shall befall on you." The boy and the girl would be hooded and driven away from the town to go and live in a hut in the bush. They would be banned from entering the town. The ban was only lifted when the girl delivered her baby. The disgrace attached to the action and the bad omen that may follow was deterrent to the youth in the

olden days therefore they shunned sex and that prevented teenage pregnancies.[209]

The Asante *asham* offering sometimes requires the rituals of hair shaving and breaking an egg on the head, this procedure is contrary to the Israelite *asham* offering.

---

[209] Osei, *A Handbook of Asante Culture*, 20.

Chapter 5: Conclusion and Recommendations

It could be concluded that even though the Israelites and Asante are similar in some of their religious ideas, they are considerably dissimilar in reality and practice. This study has revealed and confirmed that Yahweh created humans and breathed His Spirit in them. The consequence was that they were able to understand Him and the sacredness he required in the spiritual realm. This reveals and assures one that Yahweh has manifested Himself in the things He has made.

Although the Asante's religious ideas and values may in some regards be similar they are in fact very dissimilar in reality and practice. Nevertheless, the Asante rituals are very rich in concept. The value of the Asante religion is that it includes concern for truth, the human predicament, and a heart-felt religion. This creates avenues for Christians to assist the Asante to understand Yahweh far deeper just as Paul did with the Athenians in Acts 17. For this reason, this study is theologically and missiologically significant to reaching out to the Asante.

It is therefore recommended that Christians should not distance themselves from and overtly reject the Asante religious values but rather understand them in order to be able to help the Asante in the knowledge of Yahweh's salvation for mankind as revealed in Jesus Christ.

Future study should look into how some of these rich ideas and values of the Asante religion could be worked out and be applied in the propagation of the gospel in the Asante context, or elsewhere.

Select Bibliography

Adams, Frank Kwesi. *Odwira and the Gospel: A Study of the Asante Odwira Festival and Its Significance for Christianity in Ghana.* Oxford: Regnum, 2010.

Anderson, Gary A. "Sacrifice and Sacrificial Offerings" Pages 870-886 in vol.5 of *The Anchor Bible Dictionary.* Edited by David Noel Freedman, 6 vols. New York: Doubleday, 1992.

Asante, Emmanuel. "The Relationship between the Chieftaincy Institution and Christianity in Ghana." Pages 231-245 in *Chieftaincy in Ghana: Culture, Governance and Development.* Edited by Irene K. Odotei and Albert K. Awedoba. Accra, Ghana: Sub-Saharan Publishers, 2006.

Asante, Molefi Kete and Emeka Nwadiora. *Spears Masters: Introduction to African Religion.* Lanham Maryland: University Press of America, 2007.

Averbeck, R. E. "Sacrifices and Offerings." Pages 707-733 in *Dictionary of the Old Testament: Pentateuch.* Edited by Alexander T. Desmond and David Baker. Downers Grove: Intervarsity Press, 2003.

Averbeck, R.E. "āšām." Pages 557-66 in vol. 1 of New *International Dictionary of Old Testament Theology and Exegesis.* Edited by W.A. VanGemeren. 5 vols. Grand Rapids, MI: Zondervan, 1997.

Ayegboyin, Deji. "Sacrifice." Pages 583-584 in vol. 2 of *Encyclopedia of African Religion.* Edited by Molefi Kete Asante and Ama Mazama. 2 vols. Thousand Oaks: SAGE Publications, Inc., 2009.

Balentine, Samuel E. *Leviticus Interpretation: A Bible Commentary for Teaching and Preaching.* Louisville: John Knox Press, 2002.

Bellinger, W. H. Jr. Leviticus, Numbers. Vol. 3 in *New International Biblical Commentary.* Peabody, Mass: Hendrickson Publishers, Inc., 2001.

Bierlich, Bernhard, "Sacrifice, Plants, and Western Pharmaceuticals: Money and Health Care in Northern Ghana." *Medical Anthropology Quarterly* 13. 3 (1999): 316-337.

Brown, Godfrey N. *Africa in the Nineteenth and the Twentieth Centuries: A Handbook for Teachers and Students.* (Ibadan, Nigeria: Ibadan University Press, 1966.

Brown, Francis, S. R. Driver, and Charles A. Briggs, *Brown-Driver-Briggs, A Hebrew and English Lexicon of the Old Testament.* Oxford: Oxford University Press, 1907.

Busia, K.A. *The Position of the Chief in the Modern Political System of Ashanti.* Oxford: Oxford University Press, 1951.

Carpenter, Eugene and Michael A. Grisanti. "870 אשם," Pages 553-57, in vol.1 of *New International Dictionary of the Old Testament Theology and Exegesis.* Edited by Willem A. VanGemeren. 5 vols. Grand Rapids: Zondervan, 1997.

Dalley, Stephanie. *Myths from Mesopotamia: Creation, The Flood, Gilgamesh, and Others.* Oxford: Oxford University Press, 1989.

Douglas, Mary. *Leviticus As Literature.* Oxford: Oxford University Press, 1999.

Douglas, Mary. "The Forbidden Animals in Leviticus." JSOT 59 (1993), 3-23.

Duke, R. K. "Priests, Priesthood." Pages 651-655 in *Dictionary of the Old Testament: Pentateuch.* Edited by T. Desmond Alexander and David W. Baker. Downers Grove: InterVarsity Press, 2003.

Ephraim-Donkor, Anthony. *African Spirituality.* Lanham. Maryland: University Press of America, 2011.

Evans, St. John T. "The Akan Doctrine of God." Pages 241-259 in *African Ideas of God.* Edited by Edwin W. Smith. London: Edinburgh House Press, 1961.

Gane, Roy. *Leviticus, Numbers: The NIV Application Commentary.* Grand Rapids: Zondervan, 2004.

Gerstenberger, Erhard S. *Leviticus A Commentary.* Louisville, London: Westminster John Knox Press, 1996.

Glazier, Jack. "Sacrifice." Pages 1133-1136 in vol. 4 of *Encyclopedia of Cultural Anthropology.* Edited by David Levinson and Melvin Ember. 4 vols. New York: Henry Holt and Company, 1996.

Grillo, Laura S. "African Rituals." Pages 112-26 in *The Wiley-Blackwell Companion to African Religions.* Edited by Elias Kifon Bongmba. Oxford: Wiley-Blackwell, 2012.

Heusch, Luc de. *Sacrifice in Africa: Structural Approach.* Bloomington: Indiana University Press, 1985.

Hubert, Henri and Marcel Mauss. *Sacrifice: Its Nature and Function.* Translated by W. D. Hall. Chicago: University of Chicago Press, 1964.

Jensen, Adolf E. "From Myth and Cult among Primitive Peoples." Pages 175-188 in *Understanding Religious Sacrifice: A Reader.* Edited by Jeffrey Carter. London: Continuum. 2003. Accessed April 2013, EBSCOHOST e-book.

Johnston, P.S. "Life, Disease, Death." Pages 532-536 in *Dictionary of the Old Testament: Pentateuch.* Edited by T. Desmond Alexander and David W. Baker. Downers Grove: Inter Varsity Press, 2003.

Kellerman, D. "asham." Pages 429-437 in vol.1 of *Theological Dictionary of the Old Testament.* Edited by G. J. Botterweck and H. Ringgren. Grand Rapids, MI: Eerdmans, 1974.

Klingbell, Gerald A. *Bridging the Gap: Ritual and Ritual Texts in the Bible.* Winona Lake: Eisenbrauns, 2007.

Knight, George A. F. *Leviticus.* Philadelphia: The Westminster Press, 1981.

Knohl, Israel. "Between Voice and Silence: The Relationship between Prayer and Temple Cult." *JBL* 115/1 (1996): 17-30.

Lang, Bernhard. *Anthropological Approaches to the Old Testament.* Philadelphia: Fortress Press/SPCK, 1985.

Levi-Strauss, Claude. *Totemism.* Boston: Beacon Press, 1963.

Lubetski, Meir. "Medicine and Healing." Pages 659-664 in vol. 4 of *The Anchor Bible Dictionary vol. 4 K-N.* Edited by David Noel Freedman. 6 vols. New York: Doubleday, 1992.

Mbiti, John S. *African Religions & Philosophy.* New York: Praeger, 1971.

Mbiti, John S. *Concepts of God in Africa.* London: S.P.C.K, 1970.

Mbiti, John S. *Introduction of African Religion.* New York: Praeger, 1975.

Milgrom, Jacob. "Further on the Expiatory Sacrifices." *JBL* 115.3 (1996): 513-14.

Milgrom, Jacob. *Leviticus 1-16: A New Translation with Introduction and Commentary. The Anchor Bible.* New York: Doubleday, 1991.

Milgrom, Jacob. *Leviticus 17-22: A New Translation with Introduction and Commentary. The Anchor Bible.* New York: Doubleday, 1991.

Milgrom, Jacob. *Leviticus: A Book of Ritual and Ethics: A Continental Commentary.* Minneapolis: Fortress Press, 2004.

Miller, Patrick. *Deuteronomy: Interpretation, A Bible Commentary for Teaching and Preaching.* Louisville: John Knox Press, 1990.

Müller, Louise Francoise. "Dancing Golden Stools: Indigenous Religion as a Strategy for Identity Construction in Ghana." *FIR* 5.1 (2010): 32-57.

Noth, Martin. *Leviticus: A Commentary,* Philadelphia: Westminster Press, 1972.

Osei, Kwadwo. *A Handbook on Asante Culture.* Suame-Kumasi: O. Kwadwo Enterprise, 2002.

Osei, Kwadwo. *An Outline of Asante History Part 2 Volume 1.* Suame-Kumasi: O. Kwadwo Enterprise, 2000.

Parker, Simon B., ed. *Ugaritic Narrative Poetry.* Atlanta: Scholars Press, 1997.

Parrinder, Geoffrey. *African Traditional Religion.* London: Sheldon Press, 1974.

Parrinder, Geoffrey. *West African Religion.* London: The Epworth Press, 1961.

Pemberton, Glenn D. "Leviticus." in *The Transforming Word.* Edited by Mark W. Hamilton, et al. Abilene, TX: Abilene Christian University Press, 2009.

Priest, Doug Jr. *Doing Theology with the Maasai.* Pasadena, California: William Carey Library, 1990.

Prussin, Labelle. "Non-Western Sacred Sites; African Models." *Journal of the Society of Architectural Historians* 58. 3 (1991/2000): 424-433.

Rendtorff, Rolf. "Is It Possible To Read Leviticus As A Separate Book?" Pages 22-35 in *Reading Leviticus with Mary Douglas.* Edited by John F.A. Sawyer. Sheffield: Sheffield Academic Press, 1996.

Romerowski, Sylvain. "Old Testament Sacrifices and Reconciliation." *European Journal of Theology* 16 (2006): 13-24.

Rothkoff, Aaron. "Sacrifice." Pages 639-649 in vol. 17 of *Encyclopedia Judaica.* Edited by Fred Skolnik 22 vols. New York: Thomson Gale, 2007.

Routledge, Robin. "Prayer, Sacrifice and forgiveness." *European Journal of Theology* 18 (2009): 17-28.

Sarpong, Peter. *Ancestral Stool Veneration in Asante.* Kumasi, Ghana: Good shepherd Publishers Ltd., 2011.

Sarpong, Peter. *Ghana in Retrospect: Some Aspect of Ghanaian Culture.* Tema, Ghana: Ghana Publishing Corporation, 1974.

Sarpong, Peter. *Girls' Nubility Rites in Ashanti.* Tema: Ghana Publishing Corporation, 1977.

Sarpong, Peter K. *Odd Customs, Stereotypes and Prejudices.* Accra-Ghana: Sub-Saharan, 2012.

Snaith, Norman D. D. *Mercy and Sacrifice.* London: SCM press Ltd., 1953.

Sybertz, J. Healey, D. *Towards an African Narrative Theology.* New York: Orbis Books, 1996.

Thorpe, S. A. *African Traditional Religion: An Introduction.* Pretoria: University of South Africa, 1991.

Ubrurhe, J.O. "The African Concept of Sacrifice: A Starting Point of Inculturation." *African Ecclesial Review* 40. 4 (1998): 203-215.

Webner, Richard P. *Ritual Passage Sacred Journey: The Process and Organization of Religious Movement.* Washington: Smithsonian Institution Press, 1989.

Weinfeld, Moshe, *Deuteronomy 1-11: A New Translation with Introduction and Commentary, The Anchor Bible.* New York: Doubleday, 1991.

Willis, Timothy M. *Abingdon Old Testament Commentary: Leviticus.* Nashville: Abingdon Press, 2009.

Wuthnow, Robert. "Religious Orientations." Pages 2382-2387 in *Encyclopedia of Sociology. 2nd ed.* Edited by Edgar F. Borgata and Rhonda J.V. Montgomery. New York: Macmillan Reference USA, 2000.

Asante Ritual Symbols and Images

Good resources for the following Asante images can be found at:
The Manhyia Palace Museum at the Asante King's Palace in Kumasi, Ghana, endorsed by Mr. Justice Brobbey, curator of Manhyia Palace Museum. Also at:
>http://en.wikipedia.org/wiki/Ashanti_Region
>http://en.wikipedia.org/wiki/Ashanti_Empire
>http://en.wikipedia.org/wiki/Ashanti_people

Figure 1 (a)

Asante Stool
(This type can be used by anyone).

Figure 1 (b)

Asante Stool
(This type can be used by anyone).

Figure 2

A blackened stool is used for Asante deceased kings and queens. (When a king or queen dies his or her spirit is invoked into the stool after a year. Anyone who touches the stool would be controlled by the spirit of the deceased king or queen).

Figure 3

The Gold stool of Asante.

Figure 4

Otumfo Nana Opoku Ware II (Asante King) in state.

Figure 5

Otumfo Nana Osei Tutu II Asantehene in a palanquin.

Figure 6

Asante altar or shrine within the temple.

Figure 7

An entrance into the Asante temple.

Figure 8

A side view of an old Asante temple.

Figure 9

The Courtyard of an Asante temple with *Nyamedua* (a tripod-handed wooden pole with an earthen pot on it representing the altar of the Supreme Being). A man standing beside the altar of Supreme Being on his left.

Figure 10 (a)

Asante Traditional Priest

Figure 10 (b)

Asante Traditional Priest

Figure 11

Asante Traditional Priestess dancing to a traditional tune.

Figure 12

Asante chief's spokesman's staff.

Figure 13

Pouring a libation at an Asante shrine.

Figure 14 (a)

Asante Sword – Akrafana

Figure 14 (b)

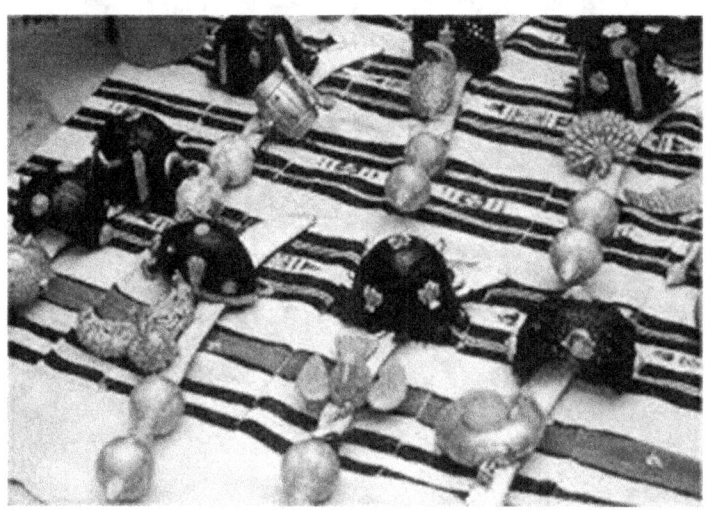

Asante royal swords.

Figure 15

Asante traditional hand-woven kente cloth designs.

Figure 16

Old Asante Palace being used as the palace museum.

HCU MEDIA LLC
Publishing in support of
Heritage Christian College – Ghana (HCC Ghana)
www.hcuc.edu.gh

HCU media has been established to support the publication of materials, both paper and electronic, created by faculty and friends of HCC Ghana. These materials are available globally.

HCC Ghana (www.hcc.edu.gh) is a Christian Liberal Arts University begun by the leadership of the Nsawam Rd. Church of Christ in Accra, Ghana with the assistance of many people, most notably the George Chisholm family and the faculty of Abilene Christian University. (www.acu.edu).

Commencing operations in September 2015, HCC Ghana offers degrees accredited by the Ghanaian National Accreditation Board (NAB) and consequently, internationally accredited bachelor degrees; in Theology, Business (Accounting, Finance, Human Resource Management, Marketing) and Information Science & Technology. HCU Ghana is affiliated with Kwame Nkrumah University of Science & Technology (www.knust.edu.gh).

Heritage Christian College Foundation USA HCCF USA (www.hccf-usa.org) was established in 2008 as a 501(c) 3 non-profit foundation with the purpose of providing donors the ability to provide needed seed capital and scholarship funding to the university. HCC Ghana intends to be a self-funding university however, in order to provide educations to needy students, scholarship funds are needed; most scholarship candidates will be orphans and ministry majors. Additionally, funding facilities requires the help of donors so that the costs of facilities do not become a burden to the tuition cost.

HCU Media LLC (www.HCUMedia.com) is the first of many entrepreneurial efforts sponsored by HCC Ghana. HCU Media is the "university press" for HCC Ghana. It will initially have offices in Plano, TX., USA and in Accra, Ghana. It will publish materials both paper and electronic which are intended to be an outlet for faculty and friends of the university.

www.ingramcontent.com/pod-product-compliance
Lightning Source LLC
Chambersburg PA
CBHW071738080526
44588CB00013B/2077